PEARLS & PROBATION

ADVENTURES OF AN ALCOHOLIC GOOD GIRL

SARAH ALAIMO

DISCLAIMER

This work is non-fiction and, as such, reflects the author's memory of the experiences. Many of the names and identifying characteristics of the individuals featured in this book have been changed to protect their privacy and certain individuals are composites. Dialogue and events have been recreated; in some cases, conversations were edited to convey their substance rather than written exactly as they occurred.

For my boys.

CONTENTS

INTRODUCTION

This is a story of a short, blonde, purpose-driven, God-loving drunk who found her strength when she woke up one morning with eight staples in her head and the determination never to drink again.

I was not supposed to end up here. My life was not supposed to turn into this. How did the absolute worst day of my life turn into the best thing that could have happened for me? I have always been a good Christian girl; this is not where good girls end up. I was raised in a good home with morals and values; this is not where good girls end up. I messed up time and time again, but this is not where good girls end up. I worked so hard my whole life to be a good, educated, faithful, loving, kind, helpful, successful woman. How did I end up in the back of a cop car, in a holding cell, in an Emergency Room on a workday, in bed with a stranger, in a hospital having my blood alcohol level drawn, in a court room with an attorney, waiting outside a probation office watching someone else get arrested, or wearing an alcohol-monitoring ankle bracelet?

None of these scenarios is where good girls end up. This was not the plan.

The plan was to get good grades, work hard in extra curriculars, and get into a good college. Upon graduation I was supposed to get married, buy a house, and start building a family. None of those other things were supposed to happen.

I had dreams of traveling, seeing the world. Learning about the Washington state judicial system was not on my list of dreams. Hiding my true life, fears, struggles, and lost ambitions also wasn't part of the scenario I'd always conjured about my future.

Addiction is choosing a drink over everything else. Recovery is choosing everything else over a drink. I guess that is how I ended up here, often in the rooms of recovery meetings, six years sober and more free, faithful, at peace, and understanding of the word serenity than I ever could have dreamed.

My Nana nicknamed me Sunshine years ago. Nana is the all-knowing, direct-VIP-line-to-God matriarch of the family. She makes friends everywhere she goes. When I moved to Washington for college we began a tradition of meeting at church, going to brunch and then doing my laundry at her house. I would stay into the evening hours, and we watched Mariner's or Seahawks games while we made dinner or ate dessert. Papa was the patriarch of the family, but even he knew who the real Captain of the ship was Nana, a.k.a Bunny, originally Laverne.

I don't know exactly when it started, but I have been her "Sunshine" for years. My aunt thought Papa came up with it, since he loved sunflowers. To my mother's horror I even got a tattoo on my left wrist in white ink to commemorate my favorite person in the world sometime around my thirtieth birthday.

I also like to think of it as carrying the sunshine with me. In the dark, extra grey months here in Seattle when I'm missing California, I can carry some of that warmth with me.

All that said, it took all of the aforementioned events for this good girl to find the strength to stop hiding and not only find, but show the world my true colors to become the sunshine in my own world.

ONE
THE JIG IS UP

THEY SAY the first step is admitting that you have a problem. I knew I had a problem. If I were being honest, I had
known for years that I was an alcoholic. Sitting in the
parking lot in the driver's seat of my beat-up Jetta, I
surveyed the situation I was about to walk into.

I had loved my previous car: a black, fully loaded
SUV. Unfortunately, she was totaled in July of 2015, back
when pride mattered more than my safety. Heck, it
mattered more than the public's safety. I lost my dear
SUV Michelle, as she was so lovingly named the night I
decided I was too cool to accept a ride from a kind male
friend of mine in hopes that he would not realize how
drunk I really was. The night I decided to take a shortcut
downtown, driving the wrong way on a one-way street.
The night I crashed into an innocent man who was simply
driving home in *his* SUV. The night I met Officer Young

(for the second time). The night that should have been my last getting drunk. But it wasn't.

The weekend prior to the wrong-way-driving incident that would put an end to my days driving Michelle through the inconsistent streets of Seattle, I tried so hard to keep my drinking at bay as I prepared for a twenty-four-hour relay race. Usually, these races were with other athlete friends, and they benefitted a charity. Given my lifestyle of regularly working out, eating healthy, and running races often, the idea that I was an alcoholic hadn't fully resonated with me. But I knew I had a problem. Having been so focused the prior week on not drinking, Monday night came along, and I was ready to meet up with my best friend Lisa for happy hour before hitting up a movie premier with a group, after which we'd have the opportunity to meet Jason Segel. Lisa and I were dangerous together. We had too much fun and were always up for one more drink. It felt so good to be out in downtown Seattle with her without a care in the world; this was the freedom Happy Hour and alcohol still gave me.

After a few drinks, Lisa left after happy hour, and I was looking forward to heading to the event with our friend, Guzman. We always had a flirtatious friendship, and I was open to seeing if it could go further. I was also secretly hopeful of catching Jason Segal's attention at the post-film meet and greet. I loved him in "Forgetting Sarah

Marshall" and "How I Met Your Mother". The night was filled with possibility.

As it turned out, Guzman was still seeing a beautiful young model he had been traveling the world with, and Jason Segel spoke, shook a few hands, and that was that. The night was a bust, but at least the crew was up for a few drinks afterward.

Guzman and I had parked in the same parking garage and given that I had consumed one too many glasses of wine, he offered to drive me home. I thanked him, and said I was fine and needed to be at work early. I also expressed concern about needing to get my car out of the garage early in the morning.

We parted ways, and while I knew it was not a great idea for me to be driving, there I was. I just wanted to get home to my dog and forget about the night altogether. As I weaved my way through the downtown streets, I found myself approaching a one-way street. Turning would take me off of my route, and I was in no mood for that. "Oh well," I thought. "It is one quick block, and no one is around. I will just proceed." So I did right into the traffic coming from my left as I tried to speed toward the next street (going the wrong direction).

The rest was a blur. After the collision, my arms were bleeding and bruised from the air bag, and my throat was sore from inhaling the chemicals that emanated from it. My ankle hurt, and I realized I must have twisted it when I slammed on the brake with my high-heeled cork wedge. I could see little else but the building I was facing, my car up on the sidewalk.

I reached for my phone, but it was dead. I could not find an insurance card in my glove box, but I was able to find my license. The rest of the details are fuzzy, but I know that I refused medical care from the EMTs. In my mind, refusing help would show them that I cared most about the other driver, and had made a simple mistake. Since my phone was dead, I was not able to produce my insurance card (I never printed it out). I was sure that was the worst part of the night, but I had no idea that Officer Young was already on his way. The one courtesy I did commit that evening was to cause this accident only one block from the police precinct, so he and other officers had a noticeably short distance to travel.

Officer Young and I were not strangers. I'd met him one year before in front of my house after, earlier that evening while at a red light, reaching over to get my coat, my car tapped the rear end of the car in front of me. When the driver came back to assess whether there was any damage, he said, "You've been drinking" and proceeded to follow me home. Without much concern, I sauntered inside and went to bed, even though he'd parked behind my car in the driveway and said he was going to call the police.

When the officers knocked on my front door, I was already asleep. After towing Michelle from the driveway, they took me to the precinct still wearing my PJs to take a breathalyzer test, which Officer Young conducted. I was blowing so hard while Officer Young screamed at me that I wasn't trying hard enough. As it turned out, the machine was broken, but my failure to make it work properly was considered an automatic refusal, so I received a DUI.

The night stretched out as I was taken into holding while a subpoena was obtained to test my blood alcohol level. We then waited for hours and hours at the local level-one trauma center for my blood to be drawn. Once the blood test was complete, Officer Young took me home with a level of grace and kindness that I did not deserve instead of booking me into the county jail while the results were pending. God sure was looking out for me, and regardless of how out of it I was, I was feeling every ounce of my white privilege in that moment.

The wrong-way collision had totaled Michelle, which is why I bought a soon-to-be-dilapidated bronze-colored Jetta a few days later. I told my family that I decided to downsize for better gas mileage. Three months after purchasing it (I never named it, hating it because it replaced Michelle), a string of bad luck unleashed itself. One evening as I was leaving the home of a guy I never intended to see again, as I tried to back out of his driveway I got stuck in the mud. I got out of the driver's seat to survey the situation, and as I did, the car rolled backwards, right down the mountain into a deep ravine of trees.

After hours of waiting for the tow truck to pull the car out, I drove home exhausted, humiliated, and $600 poorer in a car full of branches and leaves and sporting a massive dent on the left rear side. The dent would remain there until I would finally escape the curse of this evil automobile a few years later by trading it in (after narrowly escaping being rear-ended, twice). One evening, the car literally stopped out of nowhere on a freeway on-ramp during rush hour traffic.

And that is how I ended up sitting in the parking lot in the driver's seat of my run-down Jetta, six months sober, preparing to attend a recovery meeting during my lunch hour on a Tuesday.

People hurriedly made their way into the church by way of the lower-level entry. It wasn't a "basement" per se; this area is far too classy for basement meetings. Sitting there in my moniker-less car, I checked out the other attendees' clothing, bags, phones, and cars as they parked and entered. If I hadn't known this was a noon-time recovery meeting, I could easily have mistaken the crowd for a high-end downtown lunch rush.

I checked my makeup one last time. What I saw looking back at me from the mirror was a woman I barely recognized. She was tired. Tired of working so damn hard to put on a brave face and a smile every day as she took on the world. Tired of pushing away every feeling that popped into her head or heart for fear of literally losing it. Tired of putting one size-5 ½ fabulously shoed foot in front of the other. Pretty much tired of being sick and tired. This was my new normal, and that fact was still seeping its way into my hard, recently concussed skull.

I grabbed my bag and got out of the car. My office did not have a strict dress code, but lately I had been wearing at least the slacks from my suit sets on a daily basis. I have always loved a good suit; even in high school I seemed to trend towards professional-looking fashion. I had never worried this much about my clothes during these meetings until a few weeks earlier when I found myself in a downtown court room on a Saturday. Like most of the clothing, makeup, or other accessories I took the time to put on, my outfits as of late were simply there to cover up what I did not want others to see. No one outside of the committee in my head would know how carefully my attire-Sam Edelman booties, long black slacks, and a black, petite, classic Ann Taylor blazer-was chosen. Choosing a plum-colored sweater was also not an afterthought. I needed to add some color to my otherwise black uniform.

The reason I was so carefully choosing my attire these days was, six months after the wrong-way-driving debacle and five months after my last drink, I was finally arraigned and formally charged with the DUI. Because it was my second offense in as many years, the judge awarded me a beautiful alcohol-monitoring ankle bracelet. All I could say was, "At least I'm not in jail." Had Officer Young not been kind enough to take me home that night six months prior, I could easily have been stuck in jail awaiting my court date. Other than the fact that I'd avoided that nightmare, it was ridiculously hard to find a bright side to this new adornment. If you have not seen one of these ankle monitors (a SCRAM, as they are officially known), you are in good company. It reminded me of a big pager with a metal plate on the inside, kept in place by a thick, plastic tether. The metal plate was intended to be in constant contact with the wearer's skin to ensure that the monitor remained on and the individual had not consumed any alcohol.

Every night around 2am, the device's information from the day was downloaded to a centralized system, reporting in on my compliance after reading my skin for the possible presence of alcohol in my blood stream. To this day, I still occasionally experience the phantom feeling of the ankle bracelet vibrating on my left ankle.

Being petite meant that this one-size-fits-all shackle was huge and uncomfortable, and it caused daily bruising. I learned through extensive trial and error that certain shoe and sock combinations aided in keeping the contraption in place (and my ankles bruise-free). But I had to be careful with my stylish sock and shoe adjustments. If anything inhibited the metal plate from being in constant contact with my skin, it could register as non-compliant. I learned this the hard way when I chose the wrong socks/cross trainer/jogger pants combination one Saturday.

I received a call from the monitoring service a few weeks later asking what had occurred on that fateful date.

I checked my calendar and determined that I had been at a Galantines brunch with some sober sisters. I was informed that the system reported ten hours during which the monitor didn't show up as active. There was nothing the poor woman on the phone could do about it; she just wanted me to know that the courts had been notified.

I panicked and immediately reached out to my attorney as well as a sober sister who is an attorney. We decided that the best thing to do would be to present the judge with letters from everyone who saw me that day, swearing to the fact that I was wearing the monitoring device and I was not drinking.

With my court date swiftly approaching, I was terrified that this could result in the monitor remaining on longer. Or, even worse, the judge not granting me a deferred prosecution, which would allow me to be on probation for a number of years instead of going to jail, given that I was enrolled in a treatment program already.

Luckily, the judge was amazing, and she was not at all concerned about the facts of the SCRAM bracelet. She was more focused on the fact that I was able to admit that I am an alcoholic, and by that time was seven months sober, in outpatient treatment, and actively working a recovery program. She was truly the angel I needed to meet that day. I experienced a small feeling of redemption in learning that this stranger believed I could be successful in my new life as a sober, law-abiding citizen.

She finished by asking that I come back in five years

when the entire process was complete. Doing so wasn't a requirement, and only my attorney needed to be present, but coming back would show others in the courtroom what's possible.

* * *

As I made my way past the large meeting room to the smaller room in the back, I began to feel a little less nervous. I'd been attending meetings here for about six months, and I liked this smaller space. It was warm, it felt safe, and I felt like I could hide just a bit more. The smaller meeting was targeted to those of us new to the process. The meeting began promptly at noon, and all I could think about was how to sit without my thighs looking too fat or my pant leg coming up too high. By that point, I'd attended at least fifteen meetings with the monitor on and had successfully avoided anyone noticing it.

I listened as, one-by-one, each self-assured, polished speaker eloquently shared their experience, strength, and hope. I never knew what to say when it was my turn to talk. I still don't. Does anyone even care what I have to say? But I could not pass my time on this particular day; I did that too often. Realizing it was my turn, I was flushed, and my hands were shaking, I looked just over the top of people's heads so as to not make actual eye-contact while

THE JIG IS UP   11

hoping they assumed I was intentionally connecting with each and every one of them.

Finally, something came over me. I was in the middle of sharing I don't know what exactly, but I have no doubt the moment hit when it was the perfect time. With everyone watching, I slowly crossed my left leg over my right, showing off the high-heeled bootie, then pulling up the leg of my petite black Ann Taylor slacks. The room was silent for maybe two seconds before erupting into clapping, cheering, and good-natured laughter. For the first time the entire month during which I wore it, I showed someone who wasn't a close friend my ankle monitor. And not just one person either, probably thirty people! These were my people. I was home.

To this day I am approached by folks who were in that meeting or heard about it from a friend. "Hey, aren't you that girl with the ankle monitor?" they ask. I sure am! I find it funny that even in this crowd so many still get a kick out of it. I am most definitely not the first or the last person to show up to that meeting wearing such an accessory, but that day I felt like I earned some street cred and was finally starting to feel okay being part of this community.

TWO

SEEKING: PEACEFUL EASY FEELING

BEAUTIFUL, sunny, Southern California was an idyllic place to grow up. Though my parents were still in the growth phase of their shoe business when I was born, I grew up never wanting for anything I needed. I always knew I would be cared for. I was fed healthy foods, taught the major lessons of life, held to the highest standards when it came to school, and taught to try my best at the things I was not inherently great at. I appreciate the way my parents taught my younger sister and me lessons when it came to earning things in life through hard work. Learn your multiplication tables, and we will have a fantastic day at Disneyland as a family; learn to save money, and we'll match those savings for you to buy your first car. Despite that, I was constantly on the hunt for any sort of feeling of peace, no matter how fleeting. My addictive tendencies showed up on the scene long before I was old enough even to subscribe to *Cosmopolitan* magazine and learn about all the things I never knew I needed to be.

The positive lessons brought to me by my parents also carried over into trying new things. We often went to different types of restaurants. Kath, my younger sister by three years and nine months, and I were always asked to at least try everything once. We did not have to like it, but we had to try it. If we didn't enjoy a food or drink we tried, we were also asked to simply swallow it and move on. No spitting food out. Since we often tried different foods from different countries and cultures, we were taught to be polite and sensitive to new experiences. I am grateful that this example was set for us early on.

Growing up amidst the hustle and bustle of the family shoe business also provided great opportunities to learn what a strong work ethic looked like. Though this lifestyle being involved in the family business did lend itself to a somewhat nomadic childhood in comparison to our friends' families, in hindsight it was not so bad.

As young as eight, I compared myself to everyone around me to determine whether or not I was okay. I usually did not feel okay. I always felt different. *Why does everyone else seem to be so much better at life than I am? Why are things so much easier for others?* I would wonder. In response, I thought I should work harder, dress differently, lose weight, be more like someone else, and generally do anything to be better to "earn" their ease of life.

Being self-employed allowed my parents to come to

most of our school events. They chose not to put us into after-school daycare, and as a result, we were brought along with them each day after school to different stores, warehouses, and shoe factories. It was our normal, and to this day I think back on those instances both fondly and with a nagging feeling of having missed out. It was just that one other thing that made me feel different from everyone else. Our parents were more available to us from Monday through Friday; their major business days were the weekends, so my sister and I had a sitter on those days when we were younger. What I wanted was to go home after school, play on a sports team that had games on Saturdays, and go to church with my family on Sundays. I know, I sound like a spoiled brat, but don't we always want what we don't have? I yearned for the ordinary.

My mother is a conservative Christian, and my father is a liberal atheist. So, we did not really talk much about religion or politics when I was growing up. I still don't feel 100% comfortable having any sort of political conversation, however I am happy to talk about faith. This has not always been the case, but I have learned to let my heart speak for me. I cannot quote the right verse from the Bible in the moment to save my life, but I can always tell someone what I heard or read and how it made me feel and applied in my life at the time, and that is enough. After over thirty years of never feeling like I was enough, like I was right and okay, I really was seeking that precious level of approval by always trying to "do the right thing."

Who sets that standard? I still don't know, but it was an ongoing quest, another one of those things everyone else seemed to know but I thought I had to earn. I tried earning it through work, through service, through "being good," through being Christian Club President, or through saving myself for marriage. I hid from God once I chose to shed that façade, but He found me anyway!

My family moved to a nicer, more affluent area when I was in fifth grade. This was roughly the same time that those super fun changes began in my life. Puberty hit me hard! It smacked me down again and again. I started my period the day before I turned nine. I did not even know what a period was at that time. I once asked my mother what "practicing safe sex" meant when Magic Johnson tested positive for HIV and those words were all over television and radio news. She said I was too young for that conversation, and that was that. So, you can imagine how horrified I was to learn that I was going to have this horrible thing happen to me every month for the rest of my life! It was the worst day ever up until that point, at least.

In our new neighborhood we had a bigger house as well as parks and canyons nearby to explore. My sister and I started attending a new school with kids from far more affluent families than attended our previous school. I know my parents worked hard to move us to this new, safe, neighborhood, but once again, I only saw the differences between myself and everyone else my age. I had entered this new world filled with so much hope of finally fitting in. But as soon as Tyler S. made fun of my butt for "being the size of Mt. St. Helens," that hope was over. I think that move also occurred shortly before my first experience with depression. I was scared of losing my old friends and my familiar world by moving to this new neighborhood. I had a stomachache from the time we moved to the new house in May to the start of school in September.

I don't remember who it was, but I remember that just as I was starting to feel settled in with new friends and a new routine, I was made fun of for not shaving my legs yet. There began my journey to be just like all of the other girls (I cannot honestly say this is a ride I will ever fully get off of).

I made a few good friends, one who always chose to have us play at her house since it was "bigger and nicer and had furniture." She also let me borrow her clothes when I would go over to go swimming. She commented that they were much better than the ones I came over in, so I should enjoy the more expensive borrowed clothes she dressed me up in. I fully bought into this. It was likely one of the first times I started being what someone else needed me to be in order to make them happy and to fit in. "Fake it until you make it." I got darn good at that over the next twenty years!

Next, I started hanging out with the popular girls. I thought I was one of them, and I thought they liked me for me, but I also know that I never felt truly a part of that friend group. Maybe it was my weight, my clothes, the fact that I had a Walkman tape player instead of a CD player to listen to Mariah Carey on, or the reality my shorts were not short enough. Who knows?

The worst day of that year came when our teacher, Mr. P, announced that he was going to teach us how to take an average. One by one, each of us went up to the front of the classroom where he measured our height and weight. He had us write this information on the white-board along with our hair and eye color. We determined from this information that Christopher R. was the most average kid in our class when it came to height, weight, hair color, and eye color. I cannot imagine this activity being acceptable in any classroom today, and it was morti-fying. I do not remember my weight in comparison to anyone else's, but it definitely kickstarted my journey into weight loss.

I practically grew up on Weight Watchers. I remember my mother assigning labels to foods. There were only two categories: Good and Bad. And, when we were on Weight Watchers, there was also a points value assigned with each categorization. I was her diet buddy from a young age. We weathered the cabbage soup diet and fat free everything. We even hid our use of diet pills.

I carefully crafted my diet, exercise, and food restric-tion plans throughout my high school years. I had the whole process perfected early in my senior year. I had a workout system that began before my zero-period class every morning. I was then allowed a light breakfast in zero period, frozen veggies for lunch in my honor society or Christian club or yearbook editor meetings, an apple before tennis or track practice, and then a very measured usually chicken-forward dinner after hitting the gym again on my way home from practice. I really hit my stride when I could consume no more than 500 calories per day and get in at least three workouts.

As my weight decreased, a feeling of true accomplishment finally started to kick in for the first time in my life. I have always shopped in the petite section and needed a stool to reach anything, so telling you I am not tall is an understatement. But I have also always been muscular, so I do not fully identify with the medical recommendations when it comes to proper weight and height proportions. With the amount of physical activity that was a part of my daily life, a midpoint healthy weight would have been around 110 pounds. For the first time in my seventeen years on this earth, I had found something I had full control over. I continued to hone my food intake and craft the ideal workout plans. Staying busy with school work or better yet, sports activities helped to fill my time so that I didn't spend as much of it at home. Ideally, if I could miss family mealtimes, I was in a much better place not to have my lack of eating habits scrutinized.

I began to feel what resembled acceptance from others, including my mother, as my appearance began to change. I still avoided gatherings or other events as much as I could to ensure that my strict exercise routine was not disturbed (and, even more importantly, that I was not forced into a situation where I would have to eat any food that I did not deem safe). Heck, I didn't want to be in any situation where there was food at all. During this time, I often did weekend fasting or a cleanse to really kick my efforts up a notch. One of my first times trying one of these, I succeeded Saturday but was hit on Sunday with a real Sophie's Choice. As I sat in a pew in church with my friends, a challenge presented itself: Communion. Do I take the cracker and the tiny plastic cup of grape juice or not? Do I fail quietly to myself after over twenty-four hours of depriving myself was already in the bag? Or do I risk others seeing me not take part in this sacred tradition and jeopardize my standing in their eyes, in the church, and as a Christian? There was literally no good answer to this catastrophe. After minutes upon minutes of weighing my options, I ultimately took the road most travelled and opted to save face while internally screaming at the top of my lungs.

My mind was constantly filled with the details of what I would eat, what I had eaten, and even what I could have eaten but chose not to. The details of calories, quantity, portion-size, who saw me eat last, who didn't see me eat last, and on and on (and on) ravaged my brain. It never stopped. Not even with safe foods or tried-and-true measurements and confirmed caloric values.

In my mind, "safe" food meant that I was in control of what it was, how much of it I ate, and when I ate it.

Anything outside of that narrow scope could result in the necessity to work out harder the next day to burn it off or simply eliminate other foods the following day. The worst-case scenario was that one bite of something forbidden could compel me to go overboard and eat the entire thing. This was not a scenario I had an exit strategy for just yet, but the thoughts were already circulating. All or nothing was already the name of the game. And I was very poised not to let this win pass me by.

That fall, one of our cousins had a wedding our family was excited to attend. My goal weight for the wedding was eighty-three pounds. Anything less would be ideal, but this was at least a very do-able goal. I find it surprising that the goal was an odd number; I have never been one to let an odd number sit still without adding or subtracting to ensure an even-number result. This compulsion did not pertain only to food it pertained to just about anything! But I am getting off track. This was another victory. I did it! I felt amazing, albeit a little lightheaded. I was actually just under my goal weight when we left our house on Friday afternoon to head down to San Diego for the weekend of festivities. In my mind, at least, I rocked my long, size zero Jessica McClintock skirt as I manned the guest book table with gusto.

I cannot say exactly how long I kept up this level of "perfection," but eventually my family came to me as a whole and let me know I was "tearing them apart" with my disordered eating. I needed to do something about it, stat, before my problem completely ruined the family. I was horrified. I could not hurt my family! That was never my intention. I only wanted to make them proud. How could this have backfired on me so tremendously!?

I agreed then and there to do anything necessary to make them all happy again. I began seeing a therapist weekly the following week. On Wednesday nights after dinner with my family, I would take the check my mom wrote out for the visit and drive myself to a dark, warm therapist's office and try to fix myself for the sake of my family.

At first, I was incredibly uncomfortable joining this stranger. Every week, I both dreaded and looked forward to these sessions as a sort of quid pro quo with my parents. I knew I needed to go, but I never knew what to say. Was I supposed to tell her what was going on in my mind to lead me to these self-defeating thoughts? I did not have the words or the self-awareness to truly open up to the facts. I didn't want to be anything but thin, and I didn't really care how I got there. If I was choosing to hurt myself, well, that was my choice. I was angry that my family was taking it personally. Didn't they know I was doing this for them?

I lived in a state of discomfort for my entire life. Up until this point, no one had taken notice. I didn't even know that this was not the way everyone else worked. It was also not the time when I figured that out. The disappointment would simply have to continue. These sessions were not destined to provide the white-light moment in which I figured out my self-worth or the true meaning of unconditional love. I just knew something was not right. Something was missing. But what?

I do not know if these weekly visits helped or led my disordered eating journey down a new path to binging, purging, and isolation. My continued work with the therapist did, however, appease my family, and we never really talked about it again. I continued to make things look normal, but in hiding I was buying diet pills, detoxes, diuretics, and laxatives. I opted not to spend time with friends in settings I knew would be food focused. This was extremely insulating on the high school youth group circuit, where the majority of activities included sharing food, going out to get food, or hanging out at an establishment that served food.

One Friday night I opted not to go out for a friend's birthday at Ruby's on the pier because I knew I would feel uneasy in that crowd and was sick of friends always commenting on my food choices. So, I stayed home, told my friends and family I was not feeling well, and laid low watching television. I continued to obsess about the fact that I was missing out and needed something to fill that void. Finally, once the house was dark and quiet (since my sister was out and my parents had gone to bed), I decided I was hungry and needed to do something about the empty feeling.

I started with some peanut butter, which was a massive indulgence. It tasted almost too good! The

smooth, sweet, Skippy made me feel...something. I don't
know what it was, but I knew I wanted more. I made sure
to have only two spoons full again, something about even
numbers has always made me strangely comfortable. I
then moved on to a block of cheese. After that, I went
crazy and added bread into my feast. I ate and ate and ate.
I ate until I felt full and disgusting, full and fat, full and
useless. Knowing that I could have just gone out with my
friends and not gorged myself so badly, I felt instant, all-
consuming regret.

"Okay, I will take care of this," I thought. I went into
the downstairs half bath and turned the water on, making
sure to close the door quietly behind me. What I was
about to do was nearly as shameful as what I had just
done. I opened the toilet lid, put the seat up, and got down
on my hands and knees. I stuck the index finger of my
right hand to the back of my throat as far as it could go. No
luck. I then tried my middle finger with more success. I
kept this up as long as I could. Was I really failing at
purging too? I resolved to go on an extra-long run the next
day to hopefully even out the damage I had done that
night.

And thus, my new obsession began.

THREE
SHE WORKS HARD FOR THE MONEY

THE HIT SONG of the same name by Donna Summer came out the same year I was born, and it's almost like it was written with the future me in mind. Picture this: thin, blonde, conservative, business professional. Often donning a white button-up shirt with an American flag pin on the lapel and a pencil skirt. Who do you think I am describing? A Fox News anchor? Ha! This is a description of me at seventeen and eighteen, finishing out high school. My senior year I found myself listed as one of the classmates that the majority of the class of 2002 voted into a "Most likely to..." award category. The category? Most likely to be the teacher's pet. Whatever. I was honestly just so happy that people thought of me as anything special at all. I was pictured with my male counterpart, Joe, and I was, of course, dressed uber professionally. I believe they had me holding books while Joe was offering up a pile of cash.

As one of the yearbook editors, I was at least able to some-what control the narrative and make this a fun acknowl-edgement.

I discovered yearbook and photography my junior year and had a blast combining the two as the photo editor during my senior year. Junior year, I got to work with a super cute upper classman as my co-editor of sports for the yearbook, but photography was a creative outlet that I not only enjoyed but was rather good at. Maybe it was the opportunity to be behind the camera and show the world what I saw without question that appealed to me. Or, the opportunity to create something from nothing in the dark room. Not being an "artist" did not hold me back. I know it may sound self-deprecating to declare "I am not an artist," but up until that point, it was not my forte.

When I was growing up, my family and I went out to dinner a few nights a week, and every time, as we waited on our food to arrive, I would ask my dad, "What should I draw?", my crayon poised above the paper kid's menu, ready to go with whatever he suggested.

Inevitably, I was asked to draw either a horse or a dog, simply because my renderings of neither animal looked like its real-life counterpart. Since the drawings were interchangeable, it became a running joke and has since remained a funny inside Cline-family joke. No offense was ever taken.

These were also the family dinners during which I recall being allowed to stick a finger into my dad's drink to try a margarita or beer or whatever exciting concoction was served up that night. I find this interesting because my father is still a total germaphobe! Plus, I know he was worried about our family's addictive personalities. For years, he warned me about our family's addictive tendencies related to just about anything. Come to think of it, I don't remember him ever bringing this family trait up to my sister. He must have seen something "special" in me.

During my senior year of high school, my best friend Celina and I got jobs at the Turnip Rose Catering company. We were extremely excited to put on our starched white coats, black pants, bow ties, and name tags to get started working at weddings, bar mitzvahs, Seder dinners, and Quinceaneras. We had a blast and quickly made friends with the other servers, supervisors, managers, bartenders, and event coordinators we worked with each weekend. These were five-star events, so we even saw a celebrity from time to time.

I was no stranger to the concept of hard work. I liked earning my own money and the independence that it brought. The summer before college, I started working at Nordstrom during their anniversary sale. Luckily, I worked in the women's petite department. Side note: my parents actually met working at Nordstrom in Seattle. My mother had gone to school to be an English teacher, and my father had plans of becoming a veterinarian. Both changed their minds and took jobs at Nordstrom after they graduated. They met as fellow department managers and began dating. Soon after they got married, Nordstrom made plans to expand to Southern California. That is what initially took my parents from Seattle to California, but I would bet that the sunshine is what keeps them there! So, considering the idea that my sister and I are products of Nordstrom, I suppose it shouldn't be that surprising that I worked there on and off throughout college. In addition to my job at Nordstrom, I took on nannying roles that I was able to pass along to my sister once I graduated and she began attending the same college. In short, I have never been afraid of hard work. And it's a good thing.

FOUR

LIFE OUTSIDE THE BUBBLE

IN THE FALL OF 2002, my mom and I hit the road to move me into my new college dorm room at Seattle Pacific University. I was full of excitement. This was the fresh start I was ready for. I had already met my roommate from Colorado the month prior when she came to visit me. I knew we were going to have fun together. She seemed to truly be the life of the party, and I was so happy to have her by my side for this new beginning.

I chose to live in Ashton, the "party" dorm. My mother had lived in this dorm her freshman year, as had many other members of our family over the years. I was filled with anticipation to attend a school that held so much of my family's history, and to be in Seattle. I'd be close to my grandparents and other family on my mom's side who I did not get to grow up with, and both of these opportunities played into my decision to choose this school.

A few weeks into the fall quarter, my roommate invited me to come with her to a football game and frat party at another little private school that her best friend was attending in Tacoma. She was prepared with a bottle of mandarin vodka, and we grabbed sodas on the way down. This was the first time I really remember drinking and feeling its effects. Up until then, I had tried a sip here and there of my parents' drinks and had a beer or two at a baseball game with coworkers from the catering company. During the summer leading up to college, I spent a lot of time with my colleagues from the catering company, and since they were all post-college age, they bought me drinks when we were out. Still, I don't think it ever got to the point where I was drunk or lost control.

Upon application to SPU, a "Lifestyle Expectations Agreement" had to be signed. This included a full booklet of rules around not drinking, not having sex, not doing drugs, having no member of the opposite sex in your dorm room after 10:00pm, keeping one's shoes on and feet on the floor when in the room of someone of the opposite sex, and on it went. As rumor had it, there were spies out in the community, making sure we all were following the rules. This piece of information plus the intense fear of disappointing my father kept me on the straight and narrow for the majority of the four years. But not on that particular Saturday.

The moment we arrived at the football game, the drinking began. The girls I was with assumed the role of fun, carefree party girls so easily, and I was open to doing anything to fit in, "Lifestyle Expectations Agreement" be damned! This was my chance to start the life of carefree happiness I had been searching for. Midway through the game, I needed to use the restroom, and I ran into a girl in the bathroom who looked familiar. I was fairly certain that she also attended SPU. I was horrified that she would know I was drunk, so I very awkwardly said hello and ran into a stall. I felt dizzy and not fully in control of myself. Also, like I could breathe for the very first time.

Back in the day, I had an uncanny ability to stop drinking at a certain point and actually pivot the rest of my evening into something more constructive. I eventually lost this ability, and somewhat early in my drinking career no less, but more on that later.

Later that evening, a friend of a friend who also attended this school in Tacoma offered to come pick me up, and we went to a late-night coffee shop. Though I was only drinking coffee by this point, I was still able to be more open, less guarded, less inhibited. It was a fun night during which I had no problem making witty conversation with new friends. I barely knew this guy, and he thought my state of intoxication was charming.

I am not sure if I am hazy on the details because of the amount I drank or because I perhaps blacked out later on. Maybe it was one of those things that I pushed down deep enough to forget. All I know is, I was a little ashamed (and probably still a little drunk) when I met my grandmother at church the next morning. This was, for sure, my very first hangover. Of course I experienced this at church, and holy smokes, the breakfast we had after church at a restaurant in Fremont was probably the best food I had ever eaten! I still can't believe my first true hangover meal was with my sweet Nana, the one who, ironically, had always referred to me as Sunshine.

The trajectory of my freshman year changed once I joined the crew team. Being five feet and half of an inch tall, I was the perfect height for the coxswain seat in the boat. There I got to exercise my Napoleon complex as the person responsible for the safety and success of a four-woman open weight team of rowers. I would bundle up every morning for our 4:00am practice on Lake Union with four of the strongest women I had ever met. Our team did everything together. We ate together; we hit the gym together; we all weighed in together at regattas to make sure our team hit the open weight threshold. This was not easy for the coxswain, who was nothing but dead-weight in the boat. I obsessed about this. Lifting weights with my rowers and eating with them was hard. They were putting on muscle and weight, but I needed to be doing the opposite, which was challenging when I was waking up at 3:30am, had only cafeteria food options, and was trying to live the fun college life.

I wanted to be better at purging. I wanted to be more effective at fully emptying myself of the dead weight, the extra freshman pounds, the humiliation, the feeling of never being enough, the feeling of not fitting in, the fear of dropping just one of the balls I was juggling so precisely.

One of my friends on my dorm floor had been open with me, sharing the details of her struggles with an eating disorder. She had even been hospitalized and attended residential treatments more than once before entering college. One night, I was desperate and asked her to please give me some pointers on purging. She started to but stopped herself, saying she did not want to do that to me. My poor friend. I cannot even imagine how triggering my request must have been for her.

But I did not let that stop me. It was 2003, so to the Internet I went. I started obsessing about pro-anorexia sites and reading as much as I could to punish myself. Why could I not just let myself wither away? Why was I no longer good at having an eating disorder? I wanted it to be like when I was in high school and truly had control. I would have given anything to be back there. It was time to get *this* under control, so I began to see the nutritionist on campus as well as a therapist. I did not want to live that way anymore.

There were fantastic benefits to being a member of the crew team. It was an adventure I could never have imagined. When done correctly, a crew rowing together in perfect unison is truly a sight to behold. Who knew it took so much work to get to that point? And, let's be honest, how did I end up leading this novice crew? Who threw me the keys to this shell and said, "Go"? No clue. But we were actually good. In fact, we were better than good. We never lost a race. Not once. This meant that after every regatta, I was given the pleasure of being thrown into the lake, river, or ocean depending on what body of water we were competing on that day. There is no honor in being a dry coxswain leaving a regatta. Also, who made up this tradition?!

FIVE
TAKING THE PARTY ABROAD

SOPHOMORE YEAR BROUGHT new adventures with new roommates and friend groups. As the photography editor of the yearbook, I spent all my time outside of classes and friends at sporting and other school events. This was the year I homed in on my passion for business and trying to figure out my place in the world outside of the SPU bubble.

Wait...I haven't yet told you about this bubble. The phrase "ring by spring" wafted through the halls as all of the boys and a quarter of the girls had DTRs (Define The Relationship talks) as fall classes began. Though we spoke about it in jest, there was and maybe still is a slight expectation that one would meet their future husband or wife in college, just as their parents and grandparents did. So, the goal for the girls was to get that ring on their finger by spring of senior year, if not sooner.

A school such as this did not attract nearly as many male students as it did female students. I believe the ratio at the time was four females to every one male. These odds gave the boys (did you notice I did not use the word men?) a remarkably high opinion of themselves and the opportunity to really date or not date whomever they wanted. It was a wonderful environment in which to learn, but it didn't provide any real hope when it came to meeting a romantic interest.

I didn't meet my future husband there. I did, however, meet one of my absolute best friends, Dan, early in my college career. I think we were instantly kindred spirits who both wanted to and could "walk the walk." But there was always something about each of us that would stand in the way of us being the true model Christians we outwardly portrayed, and this fact cemented our bond. Thus began our friendship, and we grew even closer after graduation as we both came into our own. He has always protected me, and I have always tried to be there for him. He is one of those amazing friends whom I may not speak with for a few months, but we always pick right up where we left off.

Junior year I was blessed with the opportunity to study abroad. My best friend Sasha and I packed up our huge suitcases and made our way to England to attend a summer program at Oxford. The summer might as well have been titled "The Good Girls take Europe."

Sasha was one of the first friends I felt that I could

truly connect with. We decorated our dorm room by hanging thong underwear to a clothesline along the perimeter, so risqué in a world of promise rings and life-style expectations. Don't worry, we were classy about it; they were all brand-new, never-worn thongs. We were so rebellious that we got piercings together in the spring. Sasha got the top of her ear cartilage pierced with a swirl of three rings, and I got my belly button pierced.

When I went home for spring break and finally showed my mother one night as I got dressed to go meet up with friends, I was shocked and quite surprised by her response to the very girlie belly button piercing. My poor mama looked like she had seen a ghost and asked me, very slowly, "Does this also mean that you do drugs?" I could not hold back the giggles. "No, Mom, I have never done drugs before in my life. Nor do I plan to!" I explained that this was what was cool and in style, and I was old enough to make the decision. I don't remember it coming up again, but the belly button ring probably caused her some sleepless nights when I headed back to school, worrying about what it really meant.

Later that summer, Sasha and I flew off for our European business school adventure. The summer course we took was taught by a professor from our university, but it was taught onsite at Oxford University, specifically Exeter College, one of the forty-five schools that make up Oxford University. The crew coxswain goddess within me was freaking out to be in the UK at one of the schools that wrote so much of the history of the sport!

We lived within the four walls of Exeter College, first established in 1314 and one of the oldest in the university. Within those four history-laden walls, we each had our own room, ate all three delicious meals in the dining hall, and went to class daily with our fellow American students to learn about international business ethics. Professor Franz taught us in the more English style of teaching where we all sat around a large table in a private library and had in-depth discussions. I liked this method far more than the American style of being lectured at. We traveled around the countryside on weekends and visited the Cotswold's and Stonehenge.

Our adventure for the following fall involved attending the International Business School in Vienna, Austria. This time, we were living in apartment-style dorms with shared kitchens on each floor. There were five of us from the US, but we quickly made friends with the others on our floor and expanded our international family to include students from China, Russia, Turkey, and Ukraine to name a few. I loved our communal mealtimes sharing our cultures' foods together.

I had a serious boyfriend back home in California during this time. He was seven years older than I was, and I bought into all of his ideas of how things should be. My family upbringing was in line with the expectations his family would have of his future wife. My heritage—

Finnish, English, and German was more than acceptable to mix with his pure-bred Hungarian background. One of the partners in his accounting firm told him to hold on to me. After all, SPU turns out great wives! We were in love, but he did not want to put a ring on it until I at least had a college degree. I think the tunnel vision he had of what accolades I was supposed to have kept me on the straight and narrow during this time. Since I had him, I was careful when I went out with all of the girls. We were all of drinking age in Europe, but for some reason I was the one making sure the other girls got home safely. I almost do not even recognize that girl as I tell you about her. I cannot believe that was me, knowing the girl I morphed into.

During my time in school there, my purebred boyfriend came to visit and presented me with a promise ring. He also showed me the engagement ring he'd bought to give me after graduation. The "promise engagement" did not last even a year. He had a courier come pick up my ring the day after he broke up with me at the beginning of my senior year. I was sad for a minute but then decided to live like the twenty-one-year-old I was. My friend Mariah took me out one night to Peso's, and I knew I had arrived.

Despite the very strict Lifestyle Expectations of the University, I was ready to go out with my new group of friends. They were a little bit older than I was, so going out to bars wasn't new for them. Peso's was a trendy Mexican restaurant by day and a major hot spot at night. Despite the Agreement all students were required to sign, this was the place to see and be seen!

As I got ready for our night out, Mariah filled me in on the backstories of those we would be meeting up with. She helped me pick out an outfit that was fun and made me feel cute rather than the typical buttoned up, preppy look the "purebred" back home preferred me in. Mariah even made sure I was ready to come home from the bar later that night by placing my bathroom trash can next to my bed, along with a water bottle. This scared me a little, but it also gave me a thrill; I was "in" with this crowd.

I quickly realized how much easier it was to make interesting small talk with people I didn't know, as one by one, the Cadillac margaritas slipped back.

I felt like death the next morning, but she taught me the ropes: hydrate, hydrate, hydrate. I had been missing out the whole time on all of this fun, working so hard to be prim and proper.

SIX

F*** IT ALL

JUNE 6, 2006, will go down as a day of infamy in my life. On 06-06-06, I finally said, "F*** it!" Well, I probably did not say it in exactly that way because I wasn't yet full-on hardcore ruined. But I'm sure I said something like that, just with a bit more restraint.

I had finished my last class and was about to graduate from the strict Methodist university with lifestyle expectations. I was also figuratively graduating from being under the thumb of my parents, at least in theory. So, I did it! I gave up the v-card to a guy who definitely was more fun and thereby, in my mind anyway, made *me* more fun than the uptight, rule-following, teacher's-pet-award-winning, zipped-up-and-perfectly-ironed young girl I'd always been. I was sure he was special; I was sure there was some sort of incredibly fun future with him, and I knew he was hot, which was pretty much all that mattered. He was going to be a Navy Seal, and I was going to be whatever he wanted me to be. That was one pattern that had definitely not been broken. The magic potion that allowed me to be who *I* wanted to be would not be available to me for many more years.

Like an actress, I played a role every day of my life. On campus, I needed to be a studious, faith-focused young woman. For my family, I needed to be that *plus* ambitious and seeking to take the next expected step in my life. For my friends, I was also trying to be all of that *minus* the studious, faith-focused parts. I was not lying to anyone else while starring in these roles. It just seemed like the way to do life. I observed others and figured that at some point I would fall into the real me, and when I did, the need for guessing and costume changes and line memorization would evaporate.

Thus began the lifestyle of fitting in a good drink or two whenever it was convenient. I learned a lot of things from that someday-Navy Seal, most notably how to make a strong drink. He had been a bartender and spoke about it like it was not only the most lucrative job in the land but also the most fun and rewarding. While I have learned not to diagnose others with my disease, it is not too hard to recognize my previous thoughts and behaviors in others. He failed out of BUDS, which is Navy Seal training, and was sent to Guantanamo Bay, never to be seen or heard from again.

I honestly do not want to write about each of the

mistakes I made after this "relationship." I have done my inventory work each time I've worked the steps of my recovery program. I will say I was just a twenty-something having fun, trying to find The One, and sometimes making poor decisions in the process. Sometimes those were fueled by alcohol. Sometimes they were intended to hurt someone else or even myself. I am not proud of everything I have done in my life, but it has brought me to who I am today, and for that I am grateful. I worked through my guilt and shame and will continue to as I keep recovery at the forefront of my life.

SEVEN
THE REAL WORLD

OUR LIVES ARE what we make them...or something like that. In 2007, I began my career as a recruiter. I found my thing, my niche. I found success and notoriety, and my first professional year set forth impossible expectations. *Of course I will continue to be promoted and get $10,000 raises; this is just how things are going to be for me,* I thought.

I found that I enjoyed business, networking, and recruiting. And when those things were mixed with a happy hour, I was even more "on." I knew how to work a room, meet people, and connect people. And I was good at it. But add in a little liquid courage, and I was great at it!

I can't pinpoint the exact day on which I had my very first drink. There were those brief tastes of my parents' drinks growing up, beer at baseball games as I approached the proper drinking age, that one drink my dad bought be on a cruise, and the warm citrus vodka and Coke from the first frat party I attended. But turning twenty-one only opened more doors to do more research.

My twenty-first birthday was quite uneventful, truth be told. My family and I went to a fancy restaurant, and I ordered a sweet drink with umbrellas and fruit adorning more of the glass than was probably necessary. My dad had to ask the waiter to please card me, just for the fun of it. Later that evening, my "older sister" Chrissy took me out to TGIFridays, where I again ordered a colorful, fruity, unnaturally brightly colored concoction. This night *was* one I remember because my high school economics teacher was also at the bar and spent the evening hitting on Chrissy. I can't blame him, she's a babe and super fun, but come on!

From that point, I was off to the races, having been introduced to the fun of the bar scene and the ease of flirting with a few drinks in me for courage. My dear friend Char and I soon discovered the AMF (Adios Motherf*****, which I swear we only ordered so that we could say the last part) and the Blake Opal. It didn't take long for me to learn what was important in these drinks and what was not. I slowly graduated to focusing more on the alcohol in the glass and less on the mixers. Though shots were not really my thing, getting to the point with as few calories as possible became the name of the game.

During the first few years of my recruiting career, I kicked ass and took names. I got used to a certain level of success and the spotlight that came with it. And yet, it took so little to push me down a few pegs. I was working for a fantastic manager who reported to the epitome of the male chauvinist pig. The first time I met him, we started chatting about tennis and how I grew up playing; I even played in the intramural league in college. He immediately let me know that if he and I were to ever play, he would serve on me so hard it would probably hurt me.

Okay, cool.

Later in my tenure with the company, he was in town visiting and I was tasked with taking him, this "leader", to visit a few of our clients in the downtown Seattle core. Living and working downtown was a lot of fun for me, and I had it down to a science. There was the daily work bag I carried during my walk into the office. Each outfit had flat, more comfortable shoes for the trip to and from the office, and once I arrived, I put on the super high, super cute heels to accompany my professional attire for the day.

Anyone who has visited Seattle knows that there are a ton of hills there. I would therefore often put on flats for my walks within the city as well. On this particular day, we had a fairly good distance to cover to meet with our first client. This walk also included a bit of a hike to reach the Columbia Tower building. I met Roy outside of our street-front office, ready to impress him with the amazing relationships I had with our clients. He walked out, ready to go, looked me up and down, and began to laugh. "People take you seriously?!" He was referring to the fact that this was the first time he has seen me in flats rather than my usual heels. I was immensely proud of myself for my answer. I looked him right in the eye and confidently said, "Yes."

Luckily, his comment only gave me more motivation to kill it in those client meetings. This also was probably one of those times that I did not use my manipulative powers for good. Roy had climbed the corporate ladder in his career, and I am sure he earned his VP title. But his experience was in northern and inland California. The business climate in those areas was predominately light industrial or agricultural. I am not sure he felt fully comfortable in our clients' offices atop the tallest building in Seattle or with the insane views of the Puget Sound. As a result, I carried those meetings that day. I showed him just how seriously people did take me.

EIGHT
FEAR, DRINKSERCISE, AND A PUPPY

I WAS JUST LIVING that early-twenties life. Going to work, kicking ass, taking names, going out, and having fun. That was the name of the game. No one got hurt. Just having fun, living life, and continuing to look for The One.

The old guy. The golf guy. The love languages guy. The cheater. The therapist. None of them was The One, but I sure as hell tried to make each and every one of them *into* The One. I also did my best to be exactly what they thought I should be. This meant putting up with more of those things I said I never would. I never wanted to be with someone who had previously been married and already had kids, but there I was, constantly in those relationships. I moved from relationship to relationship, making concessions and losing more and more of myself each time.

For me, FEAR equaled F*** Everything And Run. There was always the underlying fear of not being enough. For anyone. Ever. Especially myself. And yet, I lived in a world of more. How many do you want? More. How much do you need to make? More. What do you need to do to be loved? More. Sarah, are you having another drink? Yes, one more, please. All I knew is that I needed alcohol to be "okay," at least until everything really was okay. More. I wanted more. I needed more. Of everything.

Get good grades. Do well in sports. Be liked by your peers. Be respectful to teachers. Please and Thank you. Get into a good college. Find a husband. Get a good job. Make money. Be someone. That's all. No one is asking too much of me, right? But, was anyone really asking any of this of me to begin with?

I pushed that fear down, deep down, and covered it with happy hours, wine tastings, bottomless mimosa brunches and "drinksercise" (I believe my little sister coined this term to describe the way our dog-walking friends and I would fill up our to-go coffee mugs with wine or mimosas and walk the dogs around the lake). You see, I did not have a drinking problem. I was simply a social drinker. All of my friends did it.

Speaking of dog walking, I cannot believe I have made it this far without more thoroughly introducing you to the first truly amazing man in my life. The cheese to my quesadilla. The eggs to my omelet. The chicken to my pot pie. I had to use cheese, eggs, and chicken in my descrip-tion because those are among his favorite foods. Baron. Baron Von Pom to be exact. This six-pound ball of love, energy, and fury came into my life at the exact right time.

One day I was skimming through Facebook on a lunch break and saw that my dear friend Cristine posted that the breeder she got her sweet Pomeranian, Ruffles, from had just had a new litter. The breeder, who was located in the middle of Washington state, bred prized, show-dog-quality Pomeranians. She also sold them to good homes. Her brood, The Ruff Rydn Poms, was classified by this title when they would show, and her group's logo featured a baby pom on a tiny Harley Davidson motorcycle.

Her prize-winning girl, Paisley, just had puppies with another winner, Wee Man. Paisley is only four pounds, so having just two babies was not surprising. She had a girl and a boy. The girl, named Jersey, was poised to be a prize winner as well. However, the little boy was not going to be able to show since he was born with just one eye. This did not indicate any other health issues; he simply was not going to be able to join his sister on the podium.

So Vicki, the breeder, put the word out that the little boy was available at no cost to a good family who would take good care of him. The only requirement was that the new owner sign a contract declaring that they would not breed him and that, should they be unable to care for him, they would return the little guy to her.

Cristine shared the post on Facebook and asked her

network if anyone was interested in the sweet little guy. My heart instantly melted! I knew her lovable Pomeranian was a particularly good pup with a great temperament. I had no plans until that very moment to get a dog, but I instantly replied *and* texted Cristine that I was interested. She put me in touch with the breeder, and I was on my way that weekend to the Tri-Cities to meet my little one-eyed friend.

There was one other woman interested in him, but I sure hoped I was chosen for this guy. I didn't know him yet, but I had a good feeling about him. That feeling was confirmed when I walked into the house and saw my little puff ball. He had just had a bath and was not happy about it. I loved his little attitude! I got to meet his sister and his mama. Her show dog name was Paisley "'cause she drinks, swears, steals, and lies."

Two weeks later, I got to bring my sweet Baron Von Pom home to Seattle. I had Googled "black dog names" and made a list of my top choices. I had family and close friends vote on the top three: Tank, Titan, and Baron. Being a little guy, he needed a big name. Baron, low-level nobility, fit him perfectly!

He instantly took to the city dog life. He loved everyone he met on his first outing on our way home to Seattle, especially when we stopped at a winery for a quick tasting. This was his first adventure running on the grass. He immediately took to coming to happy hour with me and taking the bus to work with me. At that time, the hospital I was working for was in the midst of being acquired so times were tough. Baron honorably took on the role of Chief Comfort Officer. Folks from all over our HR floor would come by to pet the puppy before or after having to have difficult conversations.

Who knew this little ball of energy would fill so much of that void in my life? It was a lot of responsibility for a little floof. He could never have known he was taking on such a huge job in adopting a mom. He came everywhere with me: flights home to California, restaurants, festivals, farmers markets, bars, Super Bowl parties, and everywhere in between.

I have often joked about him and his buddies needing to start their own Al-A-Dog group for fur babies who have to put up with their alcoholic parents. No matter what happened in the shadows of the previous night, BVP was always there for me in the light of day the next morning to give me snuggles and kisses. He licked my tears away when I cried, and no matter what, he would always run to me when I came home, spinning in circles with excitement. He will never be able to tell me what his early years were like, but I imagine they were kind of scary. Does a dog really need to be the "guest bartender" at the Shelter Bar? Or ride in an Uber with me to hit up a happy hour spot with friends? Probably not. But he always kept his mama safe.

From Day One of sobriety, I promised my fur baby a life-long amends. And through his health challenges, including a collapsing trachea, alopecia x, three knee surgeries with a canine orthopedic surgeon, and skin mysteries requiring a canine dermatologist, I have tried to do just that for him. Today he is a sufficiently spoiled mama's boy with more Instagram followers than I have (@baronvonpom). He belongs to an awesome Pomeranian meet-up group where he eats treats and shares water with his best friends.

NINE

AMENDS

I HAD HUMBLY ASKED God to remove my shortcomings and do with my life as He would. What a relief! I had been "managing" this dog and pony show for thirty-one years, and look where I ended up? It was time to turn over management of this life to a far more qualified leader. Then came the fun part: Making a list of all the people I harmed.

I had learned not to be sorry anymore. I had hit the maximum number of times one human is allowed to utter that word years prior. Now that I knew better, it was time to be better. That was the general message of the amends I made to my family and friends. No excuses. Just thanking them for their support, acknowledging my regret at ever hurting them, and vowing to do better each day moving forward. This also includes any harm I might cause from that day forward. I have learned to make amends on the spot.

"I have been waiting for you to outgrow this drinking phase, but you just don't seem to be," my younger sister told me the year before I chose sobriety. Katherine is nearly four years younger and knows me too well. She always has. We were as close as sisters could be growing up. We knew one another's friends and even took part in many of the same sports and other extracurricular activities. Spending one year together in high school and another in college was quite fun. In so many ways, she has often felt like the older sibling, though God knows I have always been very protective of her.

Standing three or four inches taller, Katherine declared at a young age that once she was taller, she was the sister in charge. I laughed this off, of course. When Katherine decided to move back to Washington from California, she lived with Baron and me for a few months. We had too much fun sharing clothes, going to happy hours, having friends over, and overall living it up in the same home for the first time in years.

The thing about family is, you're always there for one another, no matter what. Well, maybe not all families, and maybe not everyone in ours, but that is the code by which Kath and I live when it comes to each other, which has been both a blessing and a curse. As I watched my dear sister establish her life in Seattle, my disease continued to take a stronger hold in my life.

Katherine eventually met her now-husband and was the happiest I had ever seen her. It was so fun to add her boyfriend to our club. He has the same sense of humor she has, and we all got on very well. As their relationship progressed, Bryan was also exposed to the Jekyll-and-Hyde nature of his future bride's family. Katherine soon began to witness my true thoughts and feelings on a near nightly basis. No longer wearing the light, elegant wrap of common decorum, my Dr. Jekyll came out in full force to tell her what I really thought about her impending nuptials.

By day, I was thrilled to bits that she had found her true love. They bought a condo and were to be married in the fall. I was elated to have the honor of standing with her as her Maid of Honor. I even got to do my absolute favorite thing in the world and plan her bridal shower. No expenses were spared. I wanted this day to be perfect for my sister. I owed her.

In the nocturnal hours after we had both consumed about the same amount of alcohol, however, another side of me emerged. She later told me it had started requiring fewer and fewer drinks to elicit this change within me. She could see it coming over my face and in my eyes as I turned into another person someone jealous, cruel, and out to make the sister she loved feel as lost and scared and shitty as she did. We hurt the ones we love the most through the comfort of thinking we can never lose them.

Little by little, I was losing my sister. The night I fell

off the boat and got a concussion, my friend called her and Bryan to come to the ER. The next day, she was so angry with me that she asked for some space. I didn't blame her. She had continued to care for me throughout it all and just wanted me to get help.

A few months into my recovery journey, I received a text message from her inquiring about the amends process and when I might be working on that step. Not being very far into the work yet, I had no idea how to answer. Early on, it felt like the simplest things in life, the ones that once would not have phased me, were truly baffling. After careful consideration and consulting every mentor and friend I had in recovery, I sent a reply letting her know that while I did regret many things, I was not yet at the amends point of the process. I confided that when I was, she would be the first to know.

I kept that promise. She was the first one I approached with my letter of amends. One Saturday afternoon we met up for some Nordstrom shopping and coffee. That meeting was an awfully long time coming. We sat down outside the Nordstrom Café, and I took out my letter to read it to her. I had spent weeks writing and re-writing the words on this piece of paper. Each word was carefully chosen and signed off on by someone who knew far more about this stuff than I did. And, while I did not feel that the words were sufficient for the pain I had caused her with fear and worry for all of those years, they were the best that were available to me.

I named my regrets and suggested how I would approach each part of my life differently moving forward, especially relationships like ours that mean the world to me. When I was finished, she waited a moment to reply. I could not breathe, and I could feel my face getting hot with fear. She said this was not the letter she was expecting. My whole world sank after hearing those words. I wanted to cry, but instead did an about-face and quickly tried to change my mindset, reminding myself that this conversation was not about me. I explained to her that this is how this step goes. I later learned that she had wanted a more comprehensive list of my harms. But again, those words were not available to me. Though she did not accept my amends that day, we moved on and continued to navigate our sister-ship through new waters.

Several months later, I received a text message from my dear sister letting me know she had listened to a podcast that caused her to develop vastly different outlook on the program I was working. Husband and wife discussed each step of the process. As a result, my sweet sister has a better understanding of the work involved in each step along the road to recovery. I will forever be grateful to Dax Shephard and Kristen Bell for this episode of "Armchair Expert." The podcast's ongoing discussions about recovery have opened the door for so many meaningful conversations between Katherine and I over the years.

TEN

PRESENCE AND SELF-AWARENESS

HAVE you ever been walking through an airport baggage claim and noticed a lone suitcase circling the carousel? Just going round and round in circles, no human within miles to claim it. Did you wonder where it came from and why no one took it? I have gone down this rabbit hole, building a story around such things in the back of my mind. It is just one of those things we do, I suppose, that we don't talk about. Everyone knows what you are talking about when you mention the analogy, but it pretty much ends there.

I have always thought I had a relatively satisfactory vocabulary. With the introduction of smart phones, Alexa, and Siri, we live in a world where we never have to wonder about a fact, a measurement, or a definition. The amount of information at our fingertips and the distance our voices can travel is amazing. And yet, there are still those things everyone knows but doesn't talk about.

A dear friend felt sick at work and ended up going home early. She could not figure out what was going on, but she felt faint and had a horrible pain in her lower back. Resting at home was not making it any better, so she called up a trustworthy friend and asked her to take her to an emergency room. She had never been to an ER or urgent care and had no idea what to expect. Upon arrival, she was hooked up to IVs, blood was drawn, and she was asked to pee in a cup. As they waited, her friend answered a call from her husband, who was checking in to see how they were doing as the nurse burst through the door and asked the recently admitted patient, "Did you know you are pregnant?" Uh no. She most definitely did not. How could she be? How were her symptoms an indicator of *that* of all things? As it turned out, she also had a horrible kidney infection.

So much for HIPAA laws! The cat was out of the bag, and she was immediately faced with a decision. The medication to clear up the kidney infection was not good for an unborn fetus. What would she like to do? Fear gripped her tightly. This was not a situation she ever planned to find herself in.

The nurse leaned in towards her and flipped her name badge around, showing her a picture of a young girl, a child that the nurse had given up for adoption years before. Sharing this story clearly brought the nurse happiness. She was incredibly proud of who the child had become. But the depth of that story only added kindling to the steadily growing fire of fear, guilt, and shame burning deep down within the horrified, newly diagnosed patient.

Once discharged with medication in hand, both ladies set out to figure out how to proceed with this new information. Two days later, the same patient now quiet, tired, sad, and contemplatively in another doctor's office. Her amazing friend held her hand. And within minutes they no longer had any riddles to solve. The biggest decision she ever had to make was finalized in mere moments.

So, it was back to life as normal, right?

She was thankful for the non-judgmental support. The past few days hadn't seemed real. Had all of that just taken place? Was it a dream? It was another one of those things that other people deal with, not her. This was never supposed to be a part of her story. This wasn't anything *she* would ever do! But she did. And she did it for a million reasons, but none of them matters. What matters is that it was her choice. She honestly believes that, to this day. Never has she judged anyone else for making that same decision, but still, she was unable to show herself the same grace.

Whomever she was becoming was a stranger. She drank to avoid the whole thing beginning the following week once she was able to consume alcohol again. And that began years of spirals of shame drinking. She told practically no one. The one good thing she did do was start seeing a counselor right away. She had to do something with that pain, sadness, thoughts of "what if," and thoughts of how it would have never worked out had she made any other decision.

This is another one of those "A" words spoken only in a hushed voice, one of those words that doesn't even have a euphemism because of its straightforward definition. It's an act that movies use code words for, like "Shmushmor-shortion." It's one of those taboo, unspoken rules of societal norms, the unmentionable. And while this young, scared woman does not recommend the experience to anyone, she would also never fault anyone for making the right decision for themselves. This no longer innocent girl had an extremely hard time sanctioning that taboo and making the conversation permissible for herself. Only once she started thinking about how bringing that "A" word out of the shadows, into the sun so that others would not have to live in that guilt, could she share openly that she did, in fact, have an abortion. That day she felt a semblance of peace.

That girl...my dear friend...was me.

ELEVEN
DANGEROUS BEDFELLOWS

I HADN'T BEEN DOING a good job of choosing great relationships, but there was one that really took me down. And it took me down hard. After months and months of betrayal, lies, and hurt, the relationship came to a head one evening in late September 2014. I am a huge baseball fan. I grew up watching the Angels of Anaheim. My once girlie, floral bedroom was covered over by baseball memorabilia by early junior high. Most young girls have posters on their walls of Hollywood heart throbs or the hottest boy band, but not this girl. I had baseball players, pennants, and stats surrounding me in my little Laura-Ashley-and-Major-League-Baseball themed bedroom.

Luckily for this baseball fan, the Angels are often in town to play the Mariners since they are in the same league. As the season was drawing to a close, the guy I was dating (whom I'll refer to as Mr. S.) suggested we hit up one last baseball game. Despite being a bit under the weather and it not being terribly convenient with my work schedule, I made it happen. Of course I did. Not only is baseball my favorite, but this was an opportunity to drink before, during, *and* after a game. It was a gorgeous, sunny day, and Mr. S. wanted to spend time with me. Score! I had never been a clingy girlfriend, but over the past year, I'd come to no longer recognize myself in that or many other areas.

By early fall, I had heard from several women via email, Facebook, and text that Mr. S. was far less than faithful to our relationship. At first, he denied it, and I wanted to believe him. I didn't want to be the girl who was not enough for her boyfriend. But this was one of those bits of news that you can't unhear. I could not shake the feeling that he was not being truthful with me, and before long, I started to see it. I asked him to stop, and he said he would try. Well, he insinuated he would try, but he eventually let me know that monogamy was not part of his nature.

I did not want to be the partner who checked his phone, asked where he was and who he was with at every turn, but I quickly became that person. He often left his personal email open on my laptop, and I could not help but look. He left his phone sitting on the kitchen counter as messages popped up. He was not concerned about being caught.

On the night it all came to a head, as I mentioned, I

was not feeling well, so I took some cold medicine. This was also during the time when I was super focused on not gaining weight, so I was eating as little as I could. Drinking was a whole different story, however. I preferred the lighter alcohol options that added the fewest calories but also had the highest alcohol percentage you know, getting the best bang for my buck! All of this mixed together created a frighteningly toxic concoction.

Since Mr. S. was similar to me in eating and drinking habits, we had a system. Sometimes we had a drink in a to-go cup on our way to the game. Sometimes we pre-gamed at a local sports bar (or two). Often, he carried flasks in the large cargo pockets of his pants. For soccer games, fans were allowed to bring in a sealed water bottle. This meant we could easily bring vodka in the flask(s) and zero-calorie sparkling flavored waters as the mixer. This combination looked innocent enough to the naked eye.

To be honest, I do not recall which plan went into action this day, but I recall having fun at the game, and getting drinks and food at a brewery across from the stadium afterward. While at the brewery and feeling courageous after cold medicine and several drinks, I chose to bring up the cheating. I am fairly sure it was the same time of night when I always brought it up. But this night, I was not letting it go.

Oddly, we drove to this game instead of taking the bus as we normally did. As he drove my car home, the conversation continued. He tried to change the subject several times, but I was not interested in playing that game anymore. By the time we pulled into my driveway, he too had had it. He took the garage door opener off of the visor above the driver's seat, began to take his house key off of my key ring, and threw my house key back at me.

As he walked down the street to his parked truck, I begged him not to drive home that drunk and that angry. I tried pulling his arm back in the direction of my house. He swatted me away like a tiny fly. My five-foot-tall frame was no match for his height and muscle mass. He finally stopped at the driver's side door of his brand new, raised, black-on-black truck and let me know he was done. He was not interested in this drama any longer, and our relationship was over. How dare *he* break up with *me*! I raged at him. As he opened the car door, I pushed him and continued yelling at him. How could he do this to me when I was the one who put up with so much from *him*?

A couple was walking past with their dog, and he tried to engage them in our argument and get them to corroborate that they witnessed me pushing him. They laughed it off and kept walking. Mr. S. then got into his truck and drove off. I went inside and passed out on the couch. I slept for hours and hours as I recovered from worrying myself sick, months of sleepless nights, and months of living in self-pity. I was exhausted.

My anger was not towards him. It was at myself. I did not recognize the woman who was okay with this lifestyle. I was ashamed for trying so hard to convince him to be who I needed him to be, as if my willingness to look the other way entitled me to his gratitude forever. I could not be mad at him for treating me any sort of way. I did not respect myself, so how could I expect others to respect me?

There were two good things that resulted from our relationship. The first was how helpful he was when I first got Baron (we were still dating at that point). Having never had a dog before, I did not know what to expect. He helped me prepare to bring the little guy home. He even suggested we bring one of Baron's stuffed animals with us, one that was about his size. When we were picking Baron up, he rubbed the porcupine stuffed animal all over his sister, Jersey, so that Baron could have that familiar smell in his crate that night when he went to sleep.

The second benefit came in the form of him introducing his good friend (whom he met at work) to my dear colleague-turned-close-friend early on in our relationship. They hit it off from the jump and married a few years later. Today, they remain close friends of mine and probably his as well. We both got to support them at their wedding and thankfully did not bring our differences to their special day.

TWELVE
NEVER WOULD I EVER...

FROM 2012 TO 2015, my friend Julie and I were awesome neighbors. We were happy to let one another's dogs out when one of us was running late getting home from work. Or borrow clothes. Or pick something up at the grocery store for the other. But our best idea as friends-turned-neighbors was our wine and vegetable diet. We decided to walk the dogs "drinksercise" style, drink wine at happy hours, or drink wine at one another's house with girlfriends on craft night. It definitely helped that we chose to eat only vegetables together for a time. The only better idea we later had was getting into hot yoga. Luckily, there was a great Mexican restaurant across the street for us to hit up afterwards for margaritas.

At first, it was all just a novelty. It took some time, but drinking eventually became a habit, and not long after that, it become a problem. As I continued to mentally move down the list of all of the things that had yet to happen in my life, my drinking became a full-blown addiction.

I did not initially think about that list in the future tense. I simply had an unwritten list in my brain that presented itself right after all those rules I was so sure I needed to live by. This list was titled "I would never..." but then, one by one, I did. I did so many things in my disease that resembled the actions of a stranger. The best I could do was push those uncomfortable feelings deep down, deep inside, and never put myself in a situation where my heart or mind or brain or gut could lead me to a place where I would evaluate my life further than surface-level details.

Recruiting, business development, and courting candidates all became my thing. I was good at schmoozing; making friends; taking people out for meals, drinks, and entertainment; and generally having a great time. It was pretty easy to work this lifestyle into every facet of my world. I could always find a friend who wanted to meet for happy hour during the week or brunch on the weekends someone who could go to brunch without choosing a spot with a great bottomless mimosa option.

I never had to drink in the morning before work because that was the time of day full of guilt and shame. Luckily, I often worked with managers and teammates who instituted a happy hour in the office or at a nearby bar. Once I hit the point where my drinking habits concerned even myself, I began to put rules and parameters in place to ensure I was *not* becoming an alcoholic. I was able to respect rules such as "Do not keep alcohol in the house." That was easy; I was always out!

Then, I graduated to "only keep wine at home," because that is classy and wine tasting is a prevalent pastime in Washington. This provided another wonderful excuse to drink often and to have wine on hand at home to fill my wine rack. Let's be honest, that rack was rarely full or holding any bottles at all for longer than a few days. I thought buying the good stuff would slow me down, but it did not. I just made myself pretend to enjoy it more since it was the "good stuff." By "good stuff," I mean more expensive than Safeway's "Buy six bottles, save 10%" deal.

Drinking always seemed like a novelty. It could have been the complete 180 introducing alcohol into my life brought about, or maybe I was always just waiting for the other shoe to drop, and the realization that I was not able to drink like other people hit me. Regardless, it was a novelty until it became a necessity. Others apparently could see this happening right in front of their faces. "Why does a switch flip for you? I can see it in your eyes," my sister once said to me. And then, that switch began to flip progressively more often. I awoke each morning with hope and good intentions, but before long I lost the ability to make my own choices.

My mind was constantly filled with the details of when I would next drink, what I would drink, and any shame from the last time I drank (you know, that I needed to drink to forget). Constantly swirling were the details of who saw me drink too much last and whom I made a fool of myself in front of as I made my plans. It never stopped.

I am incredibly lucky that alcohol was far less convenient to purchase at that time. In Washington, the only alcoholic beverages you could buy in the grocery stores were beer and wine. Everything else required a trip to the liquor store. Had I lived in the era of being able to buy almost anything and everything from the grocery store, from Amazon with two-hour delivery, or from the to-go menu from local restaurants, I would have been in real trouble. Or, perhaps I would have just found my actual bottom faster.

THIRTEEN

AS THEY SAY, HISTORY REPEATS ITSELF

IF ROLLERBLADING HAD BEEN RECOGNIZED as a real sport, I would have killed it. I eventually found running and fell in love with it. There was less pressure than there was with a team sport. I also loved tennis; it was one of the hobbies that my dad and I enjoyed together. Lakers Basketball and tennis. Growing up in beautiful, sunny, Southern California, we were able to play often. A beautiful hike through the canyons or a tennis match became our go-to when I was in high school and in the summers when I came home from college.

My dad was a pretty fantastic player in his day. He is old school. I always have loved having the cute tennis skirt, tennis underwear (for holding onto your balls, of course), and a racquet that could give me any sort of edge or upper hand. And then there was Dad, still rocking his wooden racket from back in the day. He played in his K-Swiss sneakers for years. In fact, that was his day-to-day go-to shoe. I appreciate that when he finds something he likes, something that works, he sticks with it. He even has a closet full of the aforementioned K-Swiss shoes, several pair of the same New Balance running shoes, a row of the same flannel button-up in every color. Same with his shorts and Levi jeans. I think I find some sort of comfort in that today. He has always been predictable. He has always been there for me.

He came to Washington in April 2015 after receiving multiple reports from my sister that things were not steady on my home front. He asked me if I would go to a 12-step recovery meeting with him, and I declined, saying that was not something I needed. I had it all under control. I was doing well at work, I was seeing a therapist, I was working out regularly and eating healthy. I skimmed over the fact that I was working with an attorney to ensure that my DUI was pled down to a negligent driving charge.

He knew how this whole game worked. My grandparents, his parents, were possibly alcoholics also. My father was born several years after his older siblings, so he basically grew up taking care of his mother on his own. He knew the signs of an alcoholic. He also knew I was not ready to stop, and with grace, he left it alone. But not before he told me a story about my grandmother from when he was fourteen.

From the outside looking in, others saw the son of a physician who doted on a mother he loved, a hardworking and very successful student and athlete. The reality from the inside was that he grew up taking care of his mother as her alcoholism gained traction and his connection with his father and siblings slipped away. My dad's siblings are quite a bit older than he is, and by the time he entered the picture, my grandparents were heading towards divorce.

The story that my father shared with me that evening involved an experience in his early teens, going out one evening to try to find his mother and ensure that she got home safely. I can only imagine this scene where a boy, not yet a man, was trying to take his mom home and she was not yet ready to call it a night. Both of our eyes welled up with tears as he continued the story, showing me a scar on his arm from being burned with a cigarette. She was *that* resistant to leaving the bar. All I could think was, "That is not me. That could never be me."

By the grace of God, this was not the grandmother I grew up knowing. She went on to earn her bachelors degree in her sixties. I knew Grandma for her amazing creativity, artistic skill, and amazing persistence. When I was in elementary school she suffered a major stroke and lost the use of the right side of her body. Through hard work and determination, she eventually mastered the use of her left hand and regained the ability to sew, paint, write, and feed herself. I grew up with the grandma who made our American Girl dolls clothes and even made us matching dresses. I grew up with the grandma who loved an In N' Out burger with everything on it along with a chocolate shake. And through it all, I saw her children take care of her with so much love, the same love they were raised with before alcohol took over. It is because of these lessons early in his life that my dad knew his words would fall on deaf ears until I was ready to hear them.

We cried together at my dining room table. I held his hand, thinking of him as a child, the sadness my grandmother must have been living with and the terror my brave daddy must have been experiencing.

That conversation went well, so we decided to go pick my sister up and all go out to dinner since Dad was heading home the next day. Kath, Dad, and I had a lovely dinner that night at the Ivar's Salmon House on Lake Union. I enjoyed a cedar-plank-grilled piece of salmon and a glass of something red. Just one. *See, Dad, I can easily have just one.* I don't know if it's fact or fiction that my brain wants me to remember as fact, but I have a strange feeling that he asked me if I wanted another glass at some point in that meal, and I politely declined.

He would never have thought to look at my search history on my phone or laptop, but what he would have found if he had were late night Google searches including "Am I an Alcoholic?", "Pills to make me sick if I drink alcohol", "Ways to stop drinking", and "Quiz to determine alcoholism." I didn't want to live that way, but I truly didn't know any other way. I had my life down to a science. I worked ridiculously hard to make the outside look healthy, happy, successful, and trustworthy. On the inside I was screaming for help, searching for a solution, sick and tired, full of fear and lies. I did not ever want to lie to anyone, not even myself. But it became a way of life. I was not lying to anyone else to hurt them quite the opposite, in fact. I only ever intended to hurt myself; I was trying to protect everyone else. Most of the stories I told actually reflected what I wished were the truth.

FOURTEEN
UNABLE TO HIDE

THE LAST MAN I pulled into my web of insanity was a kind, athletic, sports lover. He met me a few short weeks after DUI Number One. He saw me for exactly what I showed him: a woman who worked in healthcare because she loved it, a woman who volunteered her time with young girls to give back to the community, a woman who loved the outdoors for hiking and running, a woman who worked out often, a woman who loved sports, a woman who wanted a husband and a family and loved her friends and family. I forgot to tell him that I also worked ridiculously hard at all of those things so that I would not have to come to terms with the fact that I knew drinking was destroying my life.

I was not untruthful about who I showed myself to be. It was exactly who I thought I was and exactly who I wanted to be, and we had fun until he caught on to the act.

As a therapist working with children in a juvenile detention facility, I can only imagine he saw things in me that I thought I was doing a good job of hiding. He had to have known exactly what he was looking at.

He was concerned when he experienced me coming out of a blackout for the first time. He was worried about my health that one night I drank too much at a holiday party and ended up puking in his bathroom. He suggested active activities for us to do on weekends instead of events centered around drinking. And then, one night, he asked me not to come over drunk so often. This happened most Friday nights since he worked late, and I usually met up with girlfriends after work. Luckily, this guy was also geographically desirable, as he lived only a few short blocks from my house. So, driving over wasn't too crazy in my usual inebriated state. If need be, I could walk over (which Baron loved!).

The suggestion that I would ever purposefully show up drunk or that it occurred as often as he claimed was completely offensive to me. How dare he? Was it my fault he chose a job where he worked odd hours so he couldn't enjoy happy hour with friends? Was it my fault that my friends were more fun than his and enjoyed getting together often? Was it my fault that I made more money than he did and could afford to go out with my friends? This last one was a doozy! I know I never said it out loud to him, but his mother brought it up often, so of course it was something I worried about. Was it even a good idea for me to date someone who chose the "helping people" route in life when he could be making good money as a therapist? That was just another flaw on *his* list.

"He honestly should feel lucky to be with me!" I reflected. He should feel lucky that I was fitting him into my world and my vision of the future. Once again, I was making concessions. There were only a few dealbreakers for me, and this was yet another instance where I was not being true to myself and was, more than likely, hurting someone else in the process. He wasn't my perfect person or the right man for me and my future (though I'm sure I wasn't fitting in with his vision for the future either).

We broke it off on Valentine's Day. I was sad, as I knew I was trying to make a square peg fit into a round hole. But I could also appreciate his maturity, self-respect, and honesty. The final thing I held onto was the fact that the weekend just before the break-up, I confessed to him in his car outside of my house that I had been giving some thought to the idea that I may be an alcoholic. He quickly dismissed my suggestion, saying he didn't think so. He probably desperately wanted to get away from me, and that was an easy way to get out of the conversation. I'm sure he never intended it, but what I heard was him basically giving me permission to drink for a few more months.

FIFTEEN

THE BEGINNING OF THE END

THE DAY I got to update my job title from Recruiting Manager to Director of Recruiting Operations, I genuinely thought would be unlike any other day. I had achieved a big title, and it gave me status. I was so proud that my hard work was paying off. *See, I am not an alcoholic! If I had a drinking problem, could I have gotten this promotion? Would I be off to run the Ragnar Relay on behalf of an amazing charity? Heck no!*

Would I spend that weekend sick as a dog for no apparent reason? Yes. I prepared so much better for that race than the first time I ran it. Granted, the year prior I was more of a daily runner, so running three legs of a twenty-four-hour relay covering 200 miles beginning at the Canadian border was no big deal. But this time, I knew what to expect. I packed accordingly, and luckily the organization our amazing team was running on behalf of had seriously hooked us up with a proper van and support along the way.

As we made our way to the starting line, I was already exhausted. I had to wake up super early, so I figured that was probably the reason. I began to feel faint, nauseous, and disoriented, but thought, "This really should be no biggie. I have completed a marathon as well as countless mud runs, half marathons, and every distance in between." I even rocked a Tough Mudder with a team of fire fighters! But Ragnar 2015 was a rough one as I experienced nausea, shaky hands, anxiety, and a massive headache. I had no idea I was going through withdrawals, having stopped drinking in preparation for the race. Nothing is smaller than an alcoholic wrapped up in herself.

Our team did well, and we raised a lot of money for the non-profit we were there to support. But I didn't have much fun. It was not until I made it home, took a shower, and met up with someone for a drink that I started to relax.

In August 2015, as I prepared for my second Geographic in as many months, I was enormously proud of myself for beginning my day with a run by the lake with a good friend. I've heard the word Geographic used several times throughout my years in recovery. Pulling a Geographic refers to an instance when one acts on the impulse to start over by moving to a new town or state instead of dealing with any internal changes. In essence, it's an attempt to "cure" ourselves by embarking on a fresh start in a new place.

I had recently moved to the eastside and was working hard to make healthy choices in my life so that things could start going my way again. I had moved with a good friend into her new home, which was saving me money on rent and time on my daily commute. Unfortunately, my drinking habits had become the topic of conversation more often than I was comfortable with, so within the first two weeks I set out to find another place to move into. I had not had a roommate in years, and this arrangement wasn't working out for me.

A new gentleman friend invited me to a birthday party for a dear friend of his on a houseboat one beautiful August afternoon. I really wanted to show up for him that day, since, the weekend prior, he'd seen me drunk as a skunk, embarrassing myself and my roommate at her housewarming party.

I prepared for the birthday party by making sure to look cute and bring snacks and a bottle of wine for us to share. I even made plans to go to church with my friend the next morning so that I would need to be responsible enough to get home safely and at a decent hour.

We were the first people to arrive to the boat for the party, and the energy felt quite awkward. My friend gave us a tour, and we got ourselves situated. Finally, others began to arrive. Everyone was amped up and excited to get out onto Lake Union and make our way over to Lake Washington.

We finally set sail, and I made every effort to meet people, chat, and be social, even though I felt so out of place. I didn't know anyone, and my friend didn't know any of them very well either. Plus, I felt like he was keeping an awfully close eye on me. Nevertheless, I was minding my manners and keeping my promise to not drink much.

When we stopped at the bottom of Lake Washington to drop anchor and get out the blow-up slide, the party really took off. We started socializing with people on other boats, and took our freshly grilled burgers and the can of beer we were sharing to the roof of the two-story house-boat. It was a beautiful spot from which to see the lake, the mountains, and the fun going on down in the party cove.

It wasn't long before we made some friends up top who adopted me and, as the boat headed back to its slip on Lake Union, they took us downstairs to share some fun shots with us. This is where the details get fuzzy. I know we all went back up top eventually, and I don't recall whether or not we had drinks once there, but it was one of those times when complete strangers decided to be best friends for life.

And then I woke up in a hospital on a bed that was being moved from a dark hallway into a very bright space with white curtains dividing up the cold, sterile room. I knew this place. I was back at the ER at Harborview, dizzy as a duck and wanting to know what was going on. The words coming out of my mouth were slow and hard to push out. Once out of my mouth, they felt fat and swollen and sounded funny.

I put my left hand on the back of my head, and it felt gooey. I brought my hand back in front of my face to investigate, and it was covered in blood. I tried to alert the nurse who had her back turned to me that something was wrong, and she assured me she was aware that my head was open and bleeding. I was told that I just had a CT scan and they were awaiting the results or something like that. I have no idea how long we were there. I have no idea how long they waited for my blood alcohol level to go down enough to put nine staples in my head. I have no idea when my friend called my sister, but there she was with her fiancée, relieved I was okay. She thanked the nurse and my friend for calling her. I asked her in those same puffy, indiscernible words to call my friend Anna to let her know I would not be picking her up for church in the morning. I couldn't blame her for not understanding my words. She thought I was talking about our Nana, whom I also often went to church with.

I don't know how long my sister and her fiancée stayed. I didn't know if she'd called my roommate, parents, or Nana at that point, but I knew she was angry with me for nearly dying. She shared with me that the doctor told her I should have died from my fall off of the houseboat onto the concrete dock below. That my 3.9 blood alcohol level should have killed me if the concussion that resulted from the fall didn't. She shared with me that a 4.0 blood alcohol level typically results in certain death. Then she left. She was too angry to be around me.

I was discharged that night. I was dizzy; tired; in pain; confused; hopped up on some sort of pain meds they gave me when they put the staples in; and still only wearing my pink, two-piece swimsuit (thankfully, I somehow still had my sweatshirt with me to use as a cover-up). My friend got us an Uber, and we made our way back to my house, where I simply got into bed and had the deepest sleep of my life.

When I woke up the next morning, all I knew was that I did not ever have to drink again. I hadn't wanted to for a very long time, but at this point, not only did I no longer *want* to, I no longer *had* to. And so the recovery journey began, then and there.

As I sat in the lobby of the local women's treatment facility a few days later awaiting my name to be called for my assessment, I scanned the room. I was still crazy dizzy from my concussion but felt somewhat normal wearing a cute summer dress. I had tied my hair back into a low bun, trying to conceal the nine staples holding the damage from my boating injury in place. I had been able to eat a bit of a bagel on the way over so that I could take a few Ibuprofen while I waited. I wondered if taking pills in front of others in the waiting area was triggering to them.

On the other side of the room, I noticed a tall, professionally dressed woman to my right with a shorter, older woman at her side. They were both so well put together that I assumed they were there to visit a patient. Since I was still not in the habit of making eye contact with anyone, I did not try to catch an eye to pass along a smile. It would be weeks before I'd be able to muster anything resembling care for anything or anyone outside of myself.

A tall, thin, kind-looking older woman finally came out and called my name. She took me into a dimly lit office on the bottom floor. She was disarming and spoke with a sweet lisp. For the first time in years, I was ready to be fully honest. I explained how I got there, acknowledged the amount I had been drinking, and shared my true desire to be a part of my own recovery. I don't remember much else about her questions, only that she then shared that I was seemingly a late-stage alcoholic and that their recommendation would be to enter the intensive outpatient program. I started that night.

Since I had stopped drinking on my own three or four days before my assessment, they suggested outpatient treatment, meaning that I would go in three nights a week to meet with a counselor and my group. I learned later that, had I not already stopped drinking on my own, they probably would have recommended an inpatient program where I would have stayed for roughly twenty-eight days. I am sure that I would have found every excuse under the sun not to do out-patient. I would have suggested that my job was at risk or that I could not miss my sister's wedding or that I could not leave Baron for that long.

That said, my sober sister Danika and I joke to this day that we missed out by not doing inpatient treatment. Obviously, I know it would not have been a real vacation, but it probably would have been nice to focus 100% on recovery for a month before re-entering the real world.

"Well, I'm screwed!" I remember thinking that Saturday at my first recovery meeting, looking around the room at the salty old men. This was what my life would be moving forward? At least my family was speaking to me, but I could not imagine ever being happy or having fun again. How on earth were these people smiling, laughing, drinking crap coffee, and talking about serenity?

The meeting ended up being pretty chill until I was asked to introduce myself. "Hello, my name is Sarah, and I am ..." At this point, I burst into tears. This may have been the moment I realized I was going to be classifying myself this way for the rest of my life. I was finally able to spit out the word alcoholic, but I was still in shock. Intellectually, I had known this fact for years. I had even spoken the word a few times on the Sunday preceding my fall from grace. But this was the first time it was following my name. Would I feel this way forever? Uttering those words made it sound so permanent, like there was no going back. This was not a dream, and I would not be waking up from it.

Afterwards, I went to the mall with my roommate and must have seen at least three people from the meeting. How strange. I wondered what the etiquette was for such a situation. Do we acknowledge one another? How anonymous should I be? I was not sure yet. I was still feeling broken, dizzy, exhausted, lost, and overall uncomfortable in my own skin.

A few days later, I was placed in my permanent group for the first part of my treatment program. These were the amazing women I would take this journey with for the next few months. What an incredible bond we shared! For most of us, this was our first rodeo. Danika and I were the only two who had not been in-patients, so we didn't know the others already. That said, we got to know one another quite well, quite quickly. Our pack of eight stuck together and supported one another within the four safe walls of the facility as well as outside of it, often attending meetings together on weekends and planning brunches and get togethers at each other's homes. We explored new hobbies together and new ways to fill the time we had all been gifted along with our sobriety.

I met some lifelong friends during this time. First, my sister, travel buddy, and retreat roommate, Danika. Remember the tall, put-together professional I couldn't make eye contact with in the lobby while waiting for my assessment? That was Danika! We quickly bonded over "meeting" that day and the fact that she had one more day of sobriety that I did.

The first thing she said to me when I introduced myself and said I recognized her from the assessment day was remarkable. I told her that I was sure she and the woman she was with must have been visiting a patient that day. She laughed, since she and her mother were there for the same reason I was. Her mother had flown up from Oregon to be with her as she figured out what was next for herself. I was secretly jealous that she was not there alone.

Danika then told me that she was sure I was there for a cocaine addiction, as she too was giving me the once-over of judgment from across the room. I laughed my head off at this one since I had never tried cocaine. Drugs are not a part of my story, aside from half of a pot cookie one night after a Sounders soccer game. I was not a fan and never tried it again. I am grateful that I was never offered drugs in my nine-year drinking career. I am not certain I would not have tried them, but I *am* certain that I would have liked them.

The reason Danika thought I was there for cocaine addiction was that, in her mind, I was skinny. This news made my year! In a time when all I could think about was the nine staples in my head, the constant dizziness, the aches and pains all over my body from the fall, and everything else I'd put myself through, this was the ultimate pick-me-up. We have been best friends ever since. We have even been told that our noses look so much alike that our nickname for one another is "nose twin." I will take it!

It was within this fabulous group of eight women that

Danika and I found our littermate, Terry. We determined that since they both have August 22 as their sobriety date, and I have August 23 as my birth date, that that makes us littermates. We celebrate our birthdays together every year. These women taught me that it was okay to be vulnerable and that I was safe in doing so. We discovered the real "us" together.

The first night in group when Bobbi shared her story, I felt hope for the first time. Though there was plenty in her story that both shocked and amazed me mostly regarding just how much life she had lived already even though she was a few years younger than I was there were more than a few parts of her story that I related to. Some of those details I had never told anyone aside from my closest friend and my sister. Listening to her read that night about her childhood experiences and how she ended up there with us gave me a glimmer of hope that I was going to be okay. That just maybe, all of the deep, dark secrets I could never tell another soul would actually see the light of day. That just maybe, there was some hope for me after all.

As I settled into my new life, I started to look at the similarities between my new comrades rather than focus so hard on the differences. I tried different meetings and found people I could really relate to people who understood me like no one else ever had before. I started to smile a bit more. The stories people were sharing in meetings were actually hilarious. The day that I showed my noon meeting my ankle monitor and they clapped, I knew I had arrived. These were, in fact, my people. We might seem to be well-dressed professionals on the streets, but in those meeting rooms, we were seen not for our pasts but instead for how we overcame our challenges to make it there, often broken, beaten, and battered but alive and ready to admit that something outside of ourselves brought us here and that we didn't have to drink or use that day. What a relief!

Ironically, the fears I battled in early sobriety are the same fears that motivated me to drink. They are the same fears that pop into my head today. The difference between then and now comes from having the tools to deal with the fear of failure, the fear of rejection, the fear of not being loved for me, and the fear of not being enough.

In recovery, I have women I can reach out to, books to read, and tools to combat those negative narratives. But, more than anything else, what I have is the ability to get out of my own head, hand that negative self-talk script over to my higher power, and call another mortal to get the heck over myself! You know the saying: "I'm not much, but I am all that I think about"? When I get out of my head and give someone else a call or a text to see how they are doing, I end up feeling better. Is that still a little self-centered? Yep! Does it work? Yep!

SIXTEEN

EIGHT DAYS SOBER

I JOINED a small company in the year leading up to The End. I worked directly for the founder/CEO and was given every opportunity to grow. Within the first year, I was promoted to run my division, hire a team, and take the business to the next level. Our office was comprised of three separate businesses under one large umbrella. We were a family.

My boss put up with a lot in the months leading up to my eventual and lowest rock bottom. From being my first call upon arriving home after my first DUI to being my ride home a year later after a long afternoon of drinking wine at a team building event on a boat on Lake Washington, he gave me a lot of grace, to say the least.

The most impactful moment of my life in early sobriety happened when I sat down with him at a café on my first Monday morning back in the office after taking a week off to recover from my fall, concussion, and step to get into an out-patient treatment program. We had a few minutes of awkward small talk, after which we thankfully both cut to the chase when he asked me where I had been. I told him the whole truth and nothing but the truth. He was one person in my life I was always able to be honest with. I never felt any judgment from him, and this was an incredibly unique experience for me.

I let him know I was eight days sober, and his eyes filled with tears. He told me that he had been waiting for me to join him in recovery. He shared with me that, at that point, he had been sober for one year. He shared that there were multiple times over the past year when he had wanted to grab me and try to shake some sense into me.

This was the most amazing revelation I could hear. I was shocked and happy and scared and relieved and embarrassed and willing to listen to anything he was going to share with me. He and I decided that no one in the office needed to know the whole story and that he had my back with the team. That is exactly what I needed to hear, as I knew I had a large job in front of me to rebuild trust.

The next part of our conversation, however, was the real miracle. This man hired me to do a job, promoted me to run a large part of his business, had my back, had hired an attorney to save my ass a year earlier (when I'd gotten my first DUI), *and* was showing me compassion after I left the team high and dry out of nowhere the week prior. He told me that my job was to put my sobriety first. I was given full freedom to attend noon meetings daily and leave the office at a decent hour to make it to out-patient treatment in the evenings. This gave me so much courage to walk back into the office and resume my work as the director of that division.

Though so much was terrifying in the early days, it felt incredibly good to be back at work. My work had always been a happy place for me. The next hurdle was preparing for a large conference in Las Vegas three weeks later. Day 23 of sobriety was spent at that conference, and we would be hosting a wine tasting dinner for potential clients.

In the weeks leading up to the trip, I prepared with my treatment counselor and added emergency phone numbers to my cell phone at every chance I got. That way, I had plenty of women to call in case I got into a tough situation. I called the hotel and asked that they remove the minibar from my hotel room. I even looked up meetings in the area in case I had a chance to attend. The most important piece was sharing my situation with my colleague, who was set to attend this event with me. She and I had worked together for years; in fact, I'd brought her over from the previous hospital we worked for. She had taken care of Baron countless times over the years, and I was so grateful to be working with a friend.

The day I told her the whole story, she cried. Then, we cried together. Having experienced addiction in her own family, she was more than empathetic to my situation. She was proud of me, which was a whole new feeling.

Since she is not a fan of flying, we had opportunities to lean on one another to get through the trip. I could not have done it without her. I never had the desire to drink. A concussion will definitely help with that, but it was the normal, everyday, people-to-people interactions I was having to re-learn that she really helped me with.

The Las Vegas convention victory was short-lived, because I arrived home to the beginning of the wedding festivities for my little sister and her sweet fiancée. On Day 30 of sobriety, I had the honor of standing next to my sister during her ceremony as her Maid of Honor. I did not know until years later that, had I not been sober, I may not have even been welcome at this event. The gifts of sobriety were already presenting themselves.

They say recovery is an inside job, and no truer words have ever been spoken. I chose my first sponsor because she smiled at me and made me feel welcome in a meeting I had never been to. We got to work, word by word by word, with the big blue book that would change my life forever.

I have always had a close, personal relationship with God. I was just hiding from Him while I was doing all of those things I was never going to do. But He showed himself to me and brought me back from a dark, sad, scary place into the sun. Into the sunlight of the spirit. I had my spiritual awakening on the morning of August 23, 2015, when I woke up and knew that I never had to drink again. He had lifted that burden from my shoulders. I believe that my God knows my heart and knew that I was finally done. There was no lower that I could go without ending in certain death.

The real work began when I was finally able to start writing about the resentments I felt deep down. The noise in my head that kept me from peacefully falling asleep at night, not listening to the radio in the car, or always having the television on in the background. This was the work that would ensure that no matter who I ran into at the grocery store, we were good—no shame, no guilt, no discomfort.

I learned about the part I played in a lot of my pain, even where I might not have been the instigator, and I learned better ways to handle myself in the future. I was slowly learning how to be a person in recovery. With the identification of each resentment, the weight on my shoulders became a little lighter. One day, I had been sitting in traffic for a good ten minutes before I realized I was sitting in silence, just observing the world and enjoying the sunshine. I had learned a new serenity, and I understood peace.

And, all of those horrible things I had done in my past? All of the things I was never supposed to do? All of those things that girls like me don't do? I told my sponsor every single one of them, and she did not flinch once. She did not judge me. She only probed to gain greater understanding. I was then free of it all.

SEVENTEEN

SAFETY IN SUGAR

FINDING out I was being sued by the driver of the other SUV early in my sobriety was the one and only time to date that I really, *really* wanted to escape my feelings. I stood on the corner with Baron, waiting for the crosswalk sign to blink that it was my turn to cross the street. We could cross and head straight home. Or, if we headed to the right there was a pub. I could walk in, order a drink, and instantly feel something else. Alternately, if we headed left, I could walk into Walgreens and buy something else that was forbidden but far less destructive.

I chose the safer of two evils. I picked up Baron and held him tightly as I walked down the candy aisle of Walgreen's and settled on some Reese's Cups and a Diet Coke. Even this purchase felt crazy and indulgent, and I justified it to myself the entire walk home. But this indulgence, while not healthy, would at least keep me safe

another day. It would keep my fellow Kirkland residents
safe. It would keep my sobriety date intact. Playing the
tape forward to everything that just one drink at the
Juanita Pub could produce was just far more than I could
fathom in the light of day.

I would blare "Fight Song" by Rachel Patton while
sitting in my car at Juanita beach on the top of Lake Washington. Or "Sober" by Pink. Or "Stronger" by Sara Evans.
Or "Starting Over" by Macklemore. I chose pretty much
any song I could belt out at the top of my lungs. I would
visit this beach a block or so from my apartment in my first
year of sobriety. Most of the time, it was later at night
when I was heading home and not ready to be alone yet.
Sometimes I would walk out onto the pier and just cry. I
don't know if they were tears of relief, joy, hope, fear, or a
combination of all of them. They were not sad tears. They
were cathartic. Being on the water has always brought me
peace. It's my place to talk to God. The place where I feel
safe sitting in the silence. The place where I can hide out
in plain sight. A place that's all mine.

A few months ago I was listening to a podcast and one
famous actress was asking two other famous actresses what
they would like to say to their younger selves. "Oh sweetheart, so much!" one started. "First, let me start by saying
you are enough exactly the way you are. Everyone else is
'faking it until they make it' also! Do not take yourself so
seriously, and you cannot justify this by saying that no one
else is, so why are you? It is going to be okay. You are okay.

Start living your life today, it doesn't start 'when'." Just like my drinking, I always lived my life for the next day. I'd be happy when I lost ten pounds, when I made more money, when I had a boyfriend, when I found a husband, when I bought a house, or when I achieved a new level professionally. I used the exact same logic with my drinking. "I will not have to drink so much or so often when… (insert the same line of reasoning as above). I cannot pinpoint exactly when I decided that I was not enough, but I remember when I began to think that maybe I was okay and someday could be closer to nearly enough.

The first time I stood in front of a group of strangers and talked about myself with no interruptions for twenty-five minutes was the most frightening, exhausting, exhilarating, sweaty, stomach-churning, fun I had ever had. It was around year two. I was invited to speak at a clubhouse that I had only been to once. I thought this was a fantastic place to have my first speaking experience. I figured it would be easier to stand up there and share my story with strangers. And it was. But I was so worried that they were only focusing on our differences rather than our similarities. I have no idea what I said, and holy hell that twenty-five minutes went fast! I learned that night that, when I tell my story, I need to make sure I hurry up and get sober with enough time to talk about the real good stuff.

As my amazing Higher Power would have it, I have been given several opportunities since to share my story with large groups. As I have progressed through my recovery, the story has begun to sound a little different each time. Some of that can be attributed to growth and learning more about myself. It can also change depending on my audience. I like to know who I am talking to to make sure that I highlight the important stuff in my story to that specific audience. Another difference I have become aware of is how cathartic it is to tell one's story out loud to a captive audience. There have been several times that I have realizations or have even regained memories while sharing. I am always so grateful for those opportunities. One of the largest honors I have had in the past few years was speaking together with my husband. It is pretty awesome to be a part of a duo that is passionate about sharing our experience, strength, and hope to help someone else, God willing!

As I got deeper into my work with my sponsor during my early years in sobriety, I started to see glimpses of someone I had never met but felt like I already knew. She began showing up in places I least expected to see her. One sunny afternoon, she showed up in my car sitting in dead-stopped traffic along Lake Washington. Oddly, there were only the faint noises from outside the car. No radio, no music, no podcasts. When I realized she was there in the silence, I began to laugh and cry and then cry harder as I looked up into the sky with gratitude and love. I was filled with a warmth from within. Though it was a nice, warm day outside, the warmth I was feeling came from my stomach and filled me to the top of my blonde head. This warmth was pure gratitude. This warmth was love from my higher power. This warmth was a result of the constant cacophony of chatter and thoughts and guilt and shame in my head being silenced. This was the first time in my thirty-two years on this planet that the silence was not deafening, and my mind and heart were at peace. In college, I learned to fall asleep with the television on to drown out the noise from the halls of a busy dorm. As I got older, this just became commonplace as a horrible habit. Then it became necessity. I would come home and turn on the television or music right away. It was too scary to be alone with the thoughts and feelings in my head. Sometimes, music was a bad idea, especially if I was drinking. For some reason I liked to listen to songs that made me cry, and not just cry but bawl my blue eyes out. Maybe this was the only way for me to rage against the world, or maybe it was the only way I felt comfortable having a voice. Whatever the reason, music and the soundtrack of my life was starting to take a major part in my attempts at having a coping mechanism.

EIGHTEEN

THE LIST

A FEW MONTHS before I hit my final bottom, I began to see a therapist. She was referred to me by multiple girl-friends who had seen her for a large array of reasons over the years. Honestly, I do not remember what I shared with her initially about why I was there. Probably something about not being happy. I was fairly truthful with her about many things. I even shared with her a small glimpse into my relationship with alcohol.

Luckily, I was able to get an appointment with her a few days after the boating accident. By this time, I had already admitted to being an alcoholic. Both she and my attorney recommended the same local treatment facility. It turned out that she herself had been sober for years. The treatment facility she suggested was the one she went to, and she had worked there for years as well. I don't think she was surprised one bit that I came into our appointment that day broken, beaten down, and ready to surrender, to finally be honest with her about my disease.

I continued to see her throughout my first few years of recovery, but I always felt better when I was sitting in her office with her. It was the same feeling I have today when in a recovery meeting. There is honestly nothing like one alcoholic helping another, and she knew me before my life took that fateful turn. She knew so many of my friends. She knew where I was spending evenings in outpatient treatment. In a time when everything felt new, scary, and, quite frankly, hard, sitting with her was easy. I was finally being honest with her, and it felt good. There was nothing to be gained by putting on airs any longer. I took breaks from seeing her weekly when treatment or step work with my sponsor got busy.

A year or so into my sobriety, I was so happy and thankful with the trajectory of my life. I was sober, thriving, really living life. I loved my work. I had wonderful relationships with friends and family. What was missing was someone to share that happy life with Baron and me. I was just getting out of another relationship that was full of concessions and overall just wasn't healthy. After working through the details with her to learn my part in it, she gave me some homework. She suggested I make a husband list. A list of must-haves or nice-to-haves. This way, I could refer to this list in the future to ensure that I was not making too many concessions. I recalled that my sister had done this shortly before meeting her husband. Being a recruiter, this was definitely right up my alley sort of like writing a job description; the resume of my future husband.

I was not sure how to start such a list, but I began in the notes section on my phone that night. I typed in the important things and decided to return to it daily to add or delete as I prayed about it. The list took a little time to tweak and solidify. But once it was done, I did not edit it. I never shared it with anyone else after I read it to my therapist and my sister. The next time I read the list aloud was when I met the man who fit the list of twenty-eight items. And I don't mean that he was close enough to quite a few of the twenty-eight items listed; I mean that those twenty-eight must-haves were an exact description of him. Only once he too knew he fit the bill perfectly did I share it a few times with friends who were also searching themselves. Here are a few of the items on the list so that you get the idea:

1.) Loves God/Practicing believer
2.) Close relationship with family
3.) Has a best friend/close friends
8.) Wants to have children
10.) Desire to see the world
15.) A partner with traditional family values
16.) Wants to know my family/friends
17.) Can hold own in social situations
22.) Loves my dog!

27.) Handy

For the first time probably ever, I honestly believed in this list. Not only was it realistic, but I believed that I could expect a partner to bring to our relationship the equivalent of what I was. My past didn't preclude me from deserving happiness. My past didn't make me stale goods. I was ready to be someone's partner, and I was ready to meet mine!

NINETEEN

BLOW AND GO

"OKAY, ARE YOU READY?" Danika was doing me a solid and driving my newly equipped car home since my interim fully restrictive and expensive felon license was not going to be active for a few more days. As we left the installation shop with a glove box full of clean, wrapped alcohol-monitoring mouthpieces, Danika nervously exhaled as the system beeped. When the alcohol monitor registered clear, the car started and we were off. Of course, we took a quick selfie to commemorate the event.

The drive home felt like the longest three miles of our lives. When would the system again request that she blow? (The device required the driver to prove his or her sobriety at random intervals while the car was in operation.) Was someone watching us through the dash cam? And then, it happened: The beeping let us know she needed to blow to confirm her sobriety and keep the car moving. In true Danika fashion, she pulled over and gave the task her full attention. She is far more conscientious than I am. Maybe it is the attorney in her. Or maybe that is why she *became* an attorney. Either way, she once again passed the breath test with flying colors.

As we neared my house, we cautiously continued along about five miles below the speed limit. As we approached the garage, we made sure to safely park in a spot where the car would not have to be moved. Danika again brought up how that year really could have been a great time to take the bus and not worry about having a car, but I was not in a headspace to add that to the list of ways my life was changing. Plus, I had just moved to the suburbs of Kirkland. Had I still been in Seattle, taking the bus would have been a lot easier.

We then took Danika's Jeep to get dinner. I promised her Mexican food in return for her chauffeur services that evening. As we enjoyed our sodas and gooey-cheese-covered meals, it felt amazing to have someone on this journey with me who truly understood and had my back. I had felt so alone through the process, and I had finally found my person my sober-sister best friend. Maybe this whole sobriety and living a life in recovery thing was not going to be so bad after all.

There was a lot I could learn from my dear friend, but of course I did not follow her full example. As the days and weeks went along, I never once pulled over to give the blow-and-go my full attention. I recall one day in particular when I had Baron on my lap, coffee in hand, and was driving on the freeway while quickly chewing and swallowing a bite of some delicious carb just before blowing to keep the car going, remnants of food still in my mouth. Gross, yes, but it did not phase me in the least. I was told that certain mouthwash or yeasty, carb-laden foods could set the machine off due to having similar compounds as alcohol. Luckily, that never happened. I never let it slow me down. I may have spent the majority of that year driving around alone, and I might have wondered what the cars around me thought as I blew into the rectangular box with a clear mouthpiece attached to the inner workings of my still shitty Jetta, but I also did not care. I was doing the best I could with what I had.

Meeting others in my inpatient treatment group who were going through the same process was a Godsend. As part of my deferred prosecution agreement, I would attend a treatment program for two years. In reality, the latter half was just monthly group check-ins. The most interesting thing about those sessions was learning about other women's experiences with their lawyers, parole offices, the courts, and judges. Despite the fact that all of us were charged in the same state and county for the most part, the process for each of us was different. Regardless, this was a room where I was fully able to be myself. No judgment. No airs. No hiding. No masks. An even playing field for the first time in my life. It felt good.

I am not her anymore. But I learned a hell of a lot from

her. That Sarah was learning to be in acceptance. That Sarah was learning to be okay with being okay. That Sarah was laser focused on doing the absolute best she could each day and trying not to let the past or the future define her or lead her to a place of fear. That Sarah was developing into a strong woman in recovery who was going to be happy.

TWENTY
OKAY, GOD, HERE ARE THE KEYS

ONE DAY in early fall 2018, I was looking out of the window at the changing leaves on the trees, feeling the warm sun on my face. I realized that, at that moment, I had everything I needed (though this does not mean I had everything I wanted). But, at that moment, I knew that was more than enough and was washed over by a huge, warm, comforting wave of gratitude.

I had forgotten about that somewhat recently while in the midst of a break-up with yet again, big surprise the wrong guy. Sidebar: My best advice to any woman out there dating men for whom you have to make concession after concession: Believe them when they tell you who they are. Men, in my experience, rarely put on as many airs as women and will tell you pretty early on that they are not the right one for you. Don't change to fit that model. Move on and save everyone a lot of time. Your right one is out there. You have to be open to possibility, try new things, and love yourself before you can be in the right place figuratively, mentally, and spiritually to meet The One.

I digress.

I thanked God in that moment and remembered my surrender to Him, my promise to turn my will and my life over to His care. In the weeks leading up to this day, I had lost sight a bit. I was focusing on the earthly trials of moving, demands at work, getting back to self-care after a breakup, being busy with meetings, and friends. All the things. I remembered in that moment that all of this was possible because of Him.

My prayer style is very conversational. I love to have heart-to-heart or even just mundane daily life conversations with my heavenly Father as I go about my day. This afternoon in particular, I looked out at the beauty of His creation and thanked Him, with tears in my eyes, for this life. This life that was His plan for me all along. I thanked Him for bringing me to this point. I also thanked Him for knowing that I had everything I needed. I started to list my riches, starting with my sobriety and my life in recovery. My family. My friends. The hardships that were placed in my path to lead me to where I was at that moment. And for the absolute beauty of that moment.

This was another spiritual awakening for me. I, once again, turned my life over to God, to do with as He would. To lead me on the path He set out for me long before I was even born. I told Him, "I am happy with my life; I will stop seeking happiness and comfort in things outside of Him."

So, I deleted all of the dating apps off of my phone.

No more. I was happy. I vowed to focus on me and to live out God's will, doing the work He has for me, whatever it might be. I am here to serve! Well, there is prayer, there is surrender, there is leaning in to seek God's will for me, but I guess I also did need to be in a little bit of action. It was November. I vowed then and there to be single for the time being and re-visit dating in the new year.

I kept that promise until December 31 [2018] around 10:00pm when I downloaded a dating app on my phone while waiting in line to use the bathroom at the New Year's party I was thoroughly enjoying.

TWENTY-ONE

THE ONE

WARNING: Even I feel like I might barf when I hear myself telling this story. So prepare yourself. You cannot say I didn't warn you!

There he was. That guy I had seen in Kirkland meetings for the past few years. Our brief conversation on the beach earlier that day had piqued my interest in him. I knew only a little bit about him. I remembered seeing him at a meeting once, wearing a New England Patriots sweatshirt. His shares were very heartfelt. I could tell he was a Boston guy from his cute accent! And from our previous conversation, I knew he was passionate about helping others. So, when I saw him and his buddy standing at the registration table, I hurried over to check in on his friend who had been hit with Montezuma's revenge. I then asked them to come sit with my friend Dawn and me to watch the speaker.

I instantly knew this guy was different. I felt so comfortable with him. We sat shoulder to shoulder, listening to a fantastic speaker tell his? Her? story of coming into recovery. I think he was originally from Washington, but for the life of me, I can't recall. I was too excited to be sitting next to him and too afraid of my own feelings to let myself do the typical daydreaming about whether this he was The One. Deep down, I knew he was.

Who gets to meet The One *and* fall in love with him in Puerto Vallarta? Who finds their soulmate at a 12-Step conference? I was four years sober and he was seven months sober (this time around). I would never have guessed that in a million years, but there he was, being a true gentleman all night as our crazy group ventured into the downtown core of Puerto Vallarta. We hit up a crazy dance club where he made sure I got a sugar-free Red Bull and no one danced too close to me.

Walking to our next stop, he made sure to move me to the inside part of the sidewalk as our crew made its way into the romantic part of town. We hit up an awesome karaoke bar we wanted to check out. Of course, our crew needed no alcohol to rock that bar's socks off with not only singing but dancing and a show with every performance.

He sweetly held my hand, his eyes asking mine permission before he did so, as our boisterous group of loud, sober, former drunks made our way down the Malecon, along the sand and ocean back to our party van, which would drop everyone back at their hotels in the early hours of the morning.

The conference began each morning with a 7:00am meditation meeting. After three years of attending this conference, I had never once made it to that meeting or the early morning yoga, despite often having a plan to do so. John, on the other hand, made it there, hoping to see me. I met him an hour or so later for the continental breakfast, and we haven't been apart since.

We shared our first kiss that night on a moonlit beach in Sayulita. We held hands in the van the whole way back to Puerto Nuevo that night as our group chased the blood moon. Even as I write this story, I cannot believe I'm the one who got to live it. Why did we have to meet each other in another country when we lived so close to one another, attended many of the same meetings and even went to the same church? Who knows, but I suppose it was God's plan all along.

In our dating adventures, John and I planned quite a few trips to our favorite places that we wanted to share with one another. After visiting Canada, various spots around Washington and Oregon, California, Nashville, and ultimately moving in together, we hit up his home state of Massachusetts so I could meet his family and have a true East Coast, Cape Cod, Red Sox, and lobster roll summer experience.

As soon as we moved into our new place together, conversations began about getting ready for our trip to

Massachusetts. John's enthusiasm was contagious! We got serious about eating a keto diet, hitting up the gym, and tanning, and started acquiring some new summer clothes for the trip. We even got new matching luggage. I was hopeful when John took me for a manicure the day before we left town. I knew about bits and pieces of the plans before we left, but figured this was his backyard, and whatever he had planned would be awesome.

My friend Elizabeth laughed when I told her about our plans and said he was probably going to propose on our trip. While I certainly hoped this was the case, I was trying super hard not to set up any expectations. Earlier in the summer, John had made a comment about us getting engaged in the fall, which I took at face value. Nothing was particularly special about the fall, but I also didn't want to seem too pushy. I was just excited for the day he and I would officially be man and wife.

The trip finally arrived, along with nervous anticipation. It was so special to meet his family. They were immediately warm, welcoming, and completely inclusive. We set off on our Cape Cod adventures a few days into our trip. Stop number one was Martha's Vineyard. I honestly had no idea what to expect. Regardless, I was extremely excited to board the ferry and make it over to the island. It was even better than I could have expected! Beautiful greenery, gorgeous ocean views, and breath-taking bluffs. All of this plus charming buildings. It was East Coast style with a chill, laidback beach vibe.

The first day, we headed up to Aquinnah, relaxed on the beach, and caught a beautiful sunset on a mostly secluded beach while we ate a beautiful snack that we picked up from a local general store. My heart nearly melted when John suggested we buy a cute but touristy platter to eat our cheese and crackers off of. He suggested it was great a souvenir we could take home with us. I kept thinking, "Who is this guy?"

The next day, we headed in the opposite direction on the island to a recovery meeting on the beach. The locals were so inviting. We pulled up onto the sand and joined the circle. It was a fantastic meeting, and when it was over, everyone walked down to the water and hung out for some sea salt and fellowship.

After a fantastic brunch back in Edgartown, it was time to get ready for the main event. John had found a scavenger hunt for us to take part in that would give us an opportunity to see the highlights of the island. Since we would need to prove that we made it to each spot with a photo, John suggested we dress in outfits with complementary colors. I was happy to have an excuse to do my hair, makeup, and dress cute with my handsome man. We met the scavenger hunt director in the hotel lobby and were given our first clue. We made sure to bring the brochure the hotel gave us upon arrival that had a list, complete with pictures, of the island's highlights to help us on the hunt.

The first clue took us to the alpaca farm where we

found our next clue waiting just outside of the barn. We took the opportunity to visit with the alpacas and get plenty of pictures with them. I just kept thinking, "Let's get going here! This is a scavenger hunt, and I want to win!

The second clue took us to the Oak Bluff's gingerbread houses where we were to find the pink heart house. At each stop, there were beautifully prepared clue boxes for us marked with a balloon. The owner of the pink house came out to say hello to us, and I found it curious that there were no other scavenger hunt participants running into us along the way.

From there, we got to visit a local's favorite donut shop, an ancient carousel, and the Jaws bridge. We were having such a wonderful time visiting each stop, finding our clues, each with a little trinket to help with the clue for the next stop. At the Jaws bridge (famous for being in the movie Jaws), we received our final clue for the Edgartown lighthouse. How fun! I had never visited a lighthouse before.

John is nothing if not thoughtful, and throughout the day he continued to play the same songs over and over again in the car. I noticed but didn't really say anything since we were busy reading clues and seeing the sights. Finally, we found the last spot to park and made our way up to lighthouse. "Wow, this is one full-service scavenger hunt," I thought as we pulled up to the Harbor View hotel and turned off the car, cutting off the words of Scotty

McCreary's "This is it" playing on Apple music. We parked right in front, leaving our keys with the valet.

I brushed my hair and grabbed a hair tie since it was windy down on the water. We walked out on to the sandy path and made our way to the lighthouse. The "keeper" at the bottom waved us through to head up the spiraling staircase to the top of the lighthouse. At the top of the stairs, out on the railing overlooking Edgartown and the ocean and beautiful boats out on the water, there it was, the final box, with the signature balloon to identify it. Up until this box, John had let me open the boxes to read the clues. This time he said he wanted to. He opened it, handed me the "prize" inside, which was a small, white floral bouquet similar to one a bride would carry. He got down on one knee and began to read the "clue" to me. I instantly burst into the craziest, ugliest cry you have ever heard or seen.

He pulled a thin, stealthily concealed ring box out of his pocket. The most perfect ring was presented to me as I of course said yes, pulling my best friend up from his knee to give him a kiss. Immediately, I could hear cheering from the beach below. Through shocked tears I said something about hoping no one else was waiting to come up to visit the lighthouse. John let me know that would not happen since he had it reserved for the hour. He then told me to look up toward the sky where there was a drone capturing our perfect moment and informed me that scavenger hunt director, Sandy, was down on the beach with

Randi, the photographer, who was there to capture the whole thing.

As it turned out, Sandy was a local event planner who helped John flawlessly pull off this extravaganza, and Randi is a fabulous local photographer who was there to do a photoshoot with us to capture this amazing afternoon. Still in shock and happier than I could have ever imagined, we took our engagement photos right then and there. The insanely perfect day was followed by dinner at the beautiful French restaurant next to our hotel, where they had a special sweetheart table waiting for us.

Martha's Vineyard, the Edgartown lighthouse, and the Harbor View Hotel will always hold an incredibly special place in our hearts. We planned a beautiful wedding there for the summer of 2020 that we ultimately ended up needing to postpone. But out of our adventures, we made many friends on the island and it will always be a special getaway spot for us and our families. Sandy and I became good friends, as we both planned and rescheduled our weddings alongside one another. We look forward to having an amazing party back on the island as soon as possible.

Another insane bonus from the adventure came in the form of a call from a wedding magazine wanting to share our engagement story in their fall issue. We were excited for the opportunity to share our story, the way we met in recovery and how our lives were so shaped by our faith. We are so grateful for the platform recovery has given us to share our faith and our journeys through addiction to this side of sobriety.

We bought a spin bike for the corner of our living room and started making banana bread on the regular. I joined a writing group, planned, rescheduled (and then rescheduled again) my wedding. I decided on June 5, 2021 to just go for it and planned a Zoom wedding for June 12.

Fifteen family members and friends joined us in our home along with eighty-eight others who came to us via Zoom from all over the country to celebrate with us at the ceremony in our living room, with our little Swan Lake in the background. Baron served as our Ring Baron. Our dear friend Kelli offered to make us a cake. My aunt helped me choose gorgeous flowers, and John's mother arranged them beautifully. Our friend and hair stylist not only did my hair and makeup perfectly but also provided John with a perfectly tailored suit. His neighbor Cherry was able to put a bustle in my dress in one day. John's friend, Paster Jared, was able to put together a beautiful ceremony for us, having only met us via Zoom a few days prior. Our dear friend Sarah took John and crew grocery shopping at her high-end grocery store to put together a lovely spread of all of our favorite foods. Our friend Ray helped John write a song and played the guitar for our event. My cousin Emily ensured we got plenty of photos throughout the afternoon. All of our guests' photos are proof of our unique nuptials.

All of these amazing people stepping up to make the

day personal, special, and memorable. My sister even surprised me with a bridal shower the night before with a few friends, mothers, my aunt, Nana, and a cousin. It was not the event we expected or originally planned, but it was a beautiful expression of our love for one another and the love of our families and friends.

TWENTY-TWO

THE SIMPLER LESSONS

MOST PEOPLE ARE TAUGHT the simpler lessons as children, like how to play nice with others. While that was certainly true for me, I believe that even at a young age, I learned the art of manipulation. I was not going to fully accommodate someone's needs, but it appeared as though I was. This led to a lot of people knowing me, but no one knowing the *real* me.

In late January 2021, I was preparing to be done with the court and the legal side of my second DUI and the deferred prosecution process. I had just written the chapter about the cheating boyfriend earlier in the day. In my active addiction and early recovery, I dealt with most things that were not pleasant by not dealing with them. By pushing them far, far away or burying them deep inside. My court information was no different.

I searched and searched for the information on all of

the county and state websites. I reached out to Danika to see if she was able to look up the information on me. She sent me back a screen shot of four records she found under my name—four things I did not expect to see, including two speeding tickets over the previous five years (which, luckily, had been paid). Those damn traffic cams got me every time! There was one entry that I had filed for unemployment, which was true. Finally, there was one event from early 2013 where Mr. S had filed a suit in small claims court against me. I was never served with this information, and I saw that it was thrown out only weeks after it was filed.

In that moment, I felt all of the ickiness, the guilt, the shame, the deep pit in my stomach, and the heat rising to my face from what was going back and forth between anger, sadness, fear, rage, and the returning sting of betrayal. I sat with it for a few minutes. I texted my sponsor. I then had to get on a work call.

I was able to process the feelings a bit more with John, who thought it was funny that it bothered me at all since it happened so long ago. I got to speak with two women I trust and respect immensely, who understood that feeling and reminded me that I am no longer that person.

I kept thinking about that girl, the girl who drank away that sadness instead.

I felt the feelings. I acknowledged them. I moved on. I will not regret the past, nor do I wish to shut the door on it. I now comprehend the word serenity and know what a peaceful life looks like. I know what unconditional love feels like. I know what taking vows with my soulmate and best friend feels like. I know what showing up for my people feels like. I know what I deserve, and I know when to admit that I was wrong.

It took thirty-one years to get to a place where I could start looking at my character defects with a clear mind and an open heart. It took nine years from when I began drinking to when I finally hit my final bottom. It took one afternoon of discomfort for me to acknowledge this information, learn from it, and move on.

TWENTY-THREE

WHEN IT ALL COMES TOGETHER

TODAY, on this side where I have found the sunlight and the warmth and the peace and the silence, I know that, no matter what, I am going to be okay. I do not live my life in apathy, but I do not live my life in fear any longer either. I live my life in faith. I work with other women who are also in recovery. I share my story, my testimony, my truth, and my ministry without fear of judgment and without shame. Of course I could have lived my life up until this point with a few less trips to the ER or rides in a cop car, but would I be the woman I am today if that had happened? I don't know. But I no longer live my life with regret. I know that I am exactly where I am supposed to be.

With faith, with God, and with a "spiritual experience" in accordance with the 12 steps, life and my priorities just changed. It is hard to put that shift into words, but those who have experienced a similar connection with their higher power know. Those who have experienced that "spiritual awakening" as a result of their hard work know. It is like love you just know. It is a peace and a comfort and a warmth I had never experienced before that moment.

Being raised in a mixed belief home, my mother is a conservative Christian and my father a liberal agnostic. I was given the opportunity to choose the path I wanted to take. My father was not at all against my mother sharing her faith with my sister and me. In fact, we both chose that route on our own, choosing to get involved in church and also choosing to attend a private Methodist University. In fact, I believe that my father was happy with our decisions to do so. It was simply not his choice to pursue that faith.

I believe that this taught me about accepting and understanding others for where they are coming from and loving them for it regardless. In childhood, we were exposed to different cultures through my parents' work and their choice to involve us. As a result, not only did I learn about business, ethics, and relationships, I also discovered how to learn from other cultures. I believe that this helped me as I set out on my recovery journey, and this is something I am honestly just now realizing. Initially, all I wanted to see were the differences between people because it was more comfortable to rely on what and whom I already knew. Going into treatment at Residence XII, I knew I needed help and that my life needed to change, but I had no idea what that meant or what it would look like. Once I got there, met women who told my story and to whom I could fully relate, I clung to them and those relationships.

Once we grew out of those first days and weeks and months, I was forced to embrace a new community in the rooms. It took time. It took trust. It took vulnerability. And it was worth every minute. It did not take me long to understand that in my new community I could fully be myself with no judgment. This is what I had been seeking my whole life. I didn't find it with my friends, with my family, or with my church. I found it when God gave me the gift of willingness, acceptance, surrender, and relief from the bondage of self. When I am living values-forward consistently, I have my formula for living happily.

I want to feel peace, hope, serenity. I am done with fear, dread, and praying about the unknown. I want to bring trust and a hopeful heart into this year. It is hard to know what to believe. I know that I have to take that to God, my Higher Power, whom I trust with all of my heart and soul. My God, who saved me from the depths of addiction. My God, who spared my life. My God, who has so many plans for me and has been revealing them in His perfect time.

You know that old saying, "I will believe it when I see it"? John and I have a running joke, saying that old adage backwards, "I will see it when I believe it." We know the proper word order, but I think that both versions carry some truth, at least at certain times in our lives. My husband said it backwards to be funny once, and it stuck. I think that, very often, the thoughts and experiences of many can lead them to see what has been right in front of their faces the whole time when it is the right time to understand its purpose in their lives.

All of that to say that I am on this journey to figure out what I see right in front of my face. I was professionally stuck and, quite frankly, miserable last year. What did God show me? A way to help others out of that mire. So, I have embarked on my journey to become certified as a Career Happiness Coach.

My favorite part of the last fourteen years of my career in talent acquisition has been the unique opportunities to help someone find purpose, contentment, and a truly positive improvement to their lives from their work. I have also personally chased the ease and comfort of being defined by a job I love. It is fleeting, much like the comfort that comes from that first drink. I have hopped from job to job and company to company only to realize the grass is usually not greener. I was able to learn this in my personal life. I am in the process of learning this in my professional life. Now is the time to bring that to others.

* * *

Over the years, I have worn the coach's hat several different times. In college, I taught spin classes for two large chain fitness clubs. Among the many athletic endeavors I took on in my pursuit not to be an alcoholic, one of the most rewarding was coaching a girls running organization. I see my role in leading other women through the recovery process as coaching. I am not there to tell them what to do, simply to offer suggestions based on my experience.

Having been in the recruiting game for over fourteen years, I was starting to get bored. Rather, I was getting sick of not being able to fully help others. I was miserable in a role that was all about making money for someone other than myself. It wasn't even about making money for the amazing candidates I was working to place. I had had enough. And, wouldn't you know it, a woman reached out to me on the perfect day for me to learn about a solution. As a Career Happiness Coach herself, she thought I might be a good fit for her certification program. I needed this person at that moment. I was bored and hopeless in my work, and I know I'm at my best when I am busy and helping others.

So, 2021 started out in true Sarah D. Cline-Alaimo fashion. I started a brand-new job, began a certification program, joined a group where I committed to publishing a book within the year, and then just to really make sure it was me, started another professional certification course on top of it all. What an amazing shock after a full year of literally sitting around at home trying to figure out where life was taking me. It was no longer just about me. I now also had that husband I had been searching for so desperately.

As I learned more and more about coaching professionals to find their "happy" in the workplace, I could not help but draw parallels between common limiting beliefs and the way I had lived the majority of my life. Also, how often these things have come up in my life with others and how differently I handle those situations with them as opposed to how I handle them with myself. The parallels between my work with women in recovery to the thought-process behind coaching are uncanny. I have been learning that we all know the right thing to do deep down. It is not always the easy choice, nor is it always the fun choice. As a coach, it is my job to ask the questions to help an individual unlock her own power from within.

I love when day job life and evening job life coincide. That is exactly how recovery has been as well. My sponsors have not shared anything with me that is a secret or rocket science. It is simply suggestions based on what has worked for them. As a result, that is the same approach I take with the women I work with. That's what our meetings are about: sharing our experiences, strengths, and hopes.

Just beginning the new year with all of this possibility has shed a new light on living with purpose. I see the dichotomy between who I thought I was and who I turned out to be. I had big plans for myself, and being an alcoholic was not on that list. Being a professional success, getting married, buying a house, having kids, and traveling the world were my plans.

I suppose I have figured out who I am. I am now able to be one person around all people. Take it or leave it, this is who I am. Over the years, I sought therapy, counseling, self-help routines, diets, detoxes, 30-day challenges, and throwing myself into work or volunteering to try to make myself into who I was telling the world I was. Today I am a wife, proud dog mom, loving sister, gracious daughter, cousin, granddaughter, daughter-in-law, sister-in-law, homeowner, country music lover, baker, HR professional, and alcoholic. I am all of these things, all of the time. Of each of those tags, I am proud. I am no longer seeking the next job title, focusing on my criminal record, or looking to define who I am.

I am my Nana's "Sunshine." On a particularly important date leading up to my thirtieth birthday, I got the tattoo that was on my "I am turning thirty" bucket list. The white inked sunshine sits on the inside of my left wrist. While it commemorates many important things in my life, carrying the nickname given to me by my favorite human and the happiness that a sunny day brings are the major two I hold on to. Maybe someday I will share more, but for today, those are the most important.

Working a 12-step recovery program taught me how to live in the world. It taught me how to listen and see similarities in others rather than categorizing the differences. When I sat in the small, dimly lit, warm office of my counselor, Jess, I felt safe. In the first week, I heard another member of our tight-knit group read her First Step to us, and I realized that maybe, just maybe, things would be okay. She shared with full honesty the story of her thirty years, and I could hear my story in her words. Though we were different people from the outside looking in, we were the same on the inside. All of the things I was never going to tell another living soul rolled off of her tongue with ease, and it showed me the freedom that comes from being honest.

The program I work is one of honesty. At first, I thought this simply meant that I was no longer going to be making up elaborate stories to protect the innocent. But what I learned is that the secrets I was holding onto deep down in my soul were the very factors that would keep me sick. Sharing these with another human being plus my Higher Power was going to be the only way to move from the dis-ease of my current status quo to the promises of living happy, joyous, and free. And you know what? It worked! It continues to as I share these facts with others, appropriately. There truly is no judgment in these rooms.

It was extremely hard to understand at the beginning that there honestly was no judgment amongst this motley crew of misfits. We are people who would not normally mix. Yet they are now some of my favorite people in the world to do more than mix with, we do life together! Growing up in the church, I witnessed examples of how God wanted us to live. From the stories, teachings, and fellowship I also learned what was not acceptable. One of the largest reasons I fell away from church attendance in the final years of my short-lived drinking career was a perceived need to hide. My actions, choices, and justifications were not in line with the expectations of God; therefore, I needed Him not to see me that way.

What I learned on August 23, 2015 was that He saw me all along. He protected me from myself. His plan was for me to wake up that morning. Even the doctors in the ER didn't expect that. Today, I see this story as my testimony to share with others. I want all of the other self-proclaimed Good Girls to know that it is okay not to be perfect. There really is no such thing! Look what we drive ourselves to in the pursuit of elusive perfection!

In recruiting, we have a fun name for that one perfect, hard-to-find, maybe-doesn't-even-exist candidate that a hiring manager expects for super hard-to-fill positions: the Purple Squirrel. Of course, I have had the opportunity in my many years in the industry to find one or two of these unicorns, but it is hard to do and often only accomplished with true luck!

Similar to the Purple Squirrel, the attainment of the coveted "Perfection" level is elusive. It does not exist, and no one who thinks they have reached that level in the game of life can sustain it. Most importantly, who cares! There are so many more important things to this life that we live. The deliciousness of a freshly baked chocolate chip cookie, warm out of the oven. Or having a lazy day on the couch with someone you love to recharge your batteries. Even showing that so-called weakness I used to hide with my boss lady persona by asking another human being for help. The second I took off my fancy golden handcuffs that the city of Seattle and King County presented me with (more than once) and got honest with myself was the second I was given the freedom to be me.

For all of the amazing women who may someday pick up this book, this message is for you. You are seen. You are heard. You are enough. You can make it to the other side of an eating disorder. You can recover from a seemingly hopeless reliance on alcohol to cope with life. You can go back to your church or any place where you faced judgment with your head held high. You are going to be okay. Everyone else's opinion of you is none of your business. You might roll your eyes at this last sentence. Believe me, I sure did the first hundred times I heard it! But on the one hundred and first time, I believed it. Because I was living it.

Today, I have the life I always dreamed of. Is it perfect? Heck no! But I know how to deal with the big and little curveballs life throws my way. I live with a level of peacefulness in my whole body that I never experienced before my early thirties. The constant chit-chat in my head has been silenced. The overwhelming pit in my stomach only makes an appearance when my gut is leading me to make the right decision. I have not yet encountered a day, incident, or event that would be made better or easier by my taking a drink. That obsession has been lifted. Not to toot my own horn, but honestly, this is a freaking miracle.

One Christmas Eve a few years after I got sober, we were sitting in the large church I called home at the time, awaiting the evening service. I was surrounded by my nana, papa, mom, sister, brother-in-law, and dad. I do not recall what prompted it, but my dad leaned over and thanked me. I smiled and asked, "What for?" As he put his hand on my right arm, he said, "For the ability to sleep through the night now." Apparently, he was not able to for a number of years leading up to the end of my drinking days. He shared with me that he was always in fear of receiving a phone call that I had been hurt...or worse. This brought tears to my eyes as I truly saw the harm I had caused others. I genuinely thought I was only hurting myself.

TWENTY-FOUR
WHAT REALLY MATTERS

SO, why trust me on all of this? First, you have read this far, so you know that this is not a story beautifully tied up with a perfect ribbon. I wanted to make sure to tell you my story as it was. Would anyone make this stuff up?

I think one is an expert when she has comprehensive and authoritative knowledge of or skill in a particular area. She is adept, proficient, skilled, and skillful. "Expert" implies extraordinary proficiency, and often connotes knowledge of as well as technical skill.

I am an expert at drinking too much with no ability to call it quits. I am now a Recovery Advocate as I share my full story and seek to help others along the way.

I am an expert at career development, both from my own personal experiences and from helping others with theirs since 2007.

Long story short, I know nothing, and am totally okay with that.

Today I know what matters to me, that is. What matters to you is none of my business. I know those are simple concepts, but it took me over thirty years to understand them. Until the ground was swept out from under me, I was full-time concerned with what mattered to others, how others saw me, and what I needed to attain to "fit in" with the group that I believed had it all figured out. I was sure *everyone* else had it all figured out!

What I figured out was that the only thing that matters in my world is how I live in it. I have learned to seek God and His guidance always. Early on, I checked in with my sponsor often to make sure that whatever my brain was telling me to do was the proper next step. You have clearly seen why I needed to check in with an adult before I took any action in my drinking days, my best thinking got me to that bottom. And, in learning a whole new way to do life, I learned to put my recovery first, seek out my Higher Power for guidance, and ask for help when I need it. I learned that no one cares what my job is, what my yearly salary looks like, or how many LinkedIn connections I have. As long as I love my work and am able to pay my bills, nothing else matters.

I am sober, happily employed, and surrounded by love and support. This is what I have wanted for years. Time to be happy? Hell no! My first sponsor used to remind me

that "Fear robs of us our happiness." I am sober AF; I am supposed to be happy, joyous, and free!

More it's what I always wanted. More is my favorite number. I've learned that it was okay to want more out of life. I've also learned that getting more is no one's responsibility but mine.

ACKNOWLEDGMENTS

Thank you to my husband, best friend, and soulmate, John, for suggesting I join you for a memoir writing workshop. Without you, this book would never have come to fruition. Thank you for your encouragement throughout the entire process. I love you and am insanely grateful that our paths crossed.

My sister, Special-K, Lieutenant Weasel, Kath, I want to thank you so much for keeping me honest, keeping me on track, and pushing me to put the *real* stuff in this story. Thank you for being my fact checker and day-to-day editor-in-chief. I love you, kid. Grateful to have the opportunity to offer you a living amends on the daily. And thank you for Hudson J. Baby. He is my favorite!

My tribe you know who you are. The women who have been walking with me side-by-side through this journey since it began in 2015. And, to those amazing friends who have stuck with me even before recovery became a reality for me. You all have played such a key role in my daily life. No words can explain my love for you, admiration of your strength, and gratitude that I get to be a part of your journey as well.

My fur-baby, Baron. You are the best decision I made the year I brought you home to Seattle with me. Thank you for choosing me to be your human Mom. I owe you so many treats, buddy!

To Amy, who showed me that this is possible. I am not a writer, and YET here we are. I guess a few good things did come out of 2020. I love you and am incredibly grateful to have you in my life!

Thank you to all of the Good Girls out there who inspired me to put my story out. I hope you are able to find some relief in knowing you are not alone, and you will be okay. I am going to start a secret society for us just look for "GG"; someone wearing pearls will lean over for you to whisper the password in her ear.

Thank you to Anna, Heidi, Liz and the Inner Circle. Each of you played a ginormous role in making this book possible! Thank you for including me in your cool writers' gang, it means the world to me! Your encouragement throughout this process was invaluable!

Kaitlin, thank you for your ongoing support and encouragement! And for my kickass website! You are an inspiration and treasure. I appreciate all that you do for me and the other amazing BEAM babes!

Nose Twin, I love you, sister! Happy six years! I am so glad that our twisted paths crossed when they did, and we get to do this crazy thing together! I have loved every minute of our adventures together. You know I will always say yes when you call with a suggestion that is why we are so dangerous together. And I love it! I would not want to be nose twins with anyone else and will be yours forever. You know you are never getting rid of me!

Littermate Happy Birthday, my dear, sweet Terry! It has been nothing but a true pleasure to have you in my life. You have brought so much positivity and strength to my world and to Baron's world as well. Your kindness, calm nature, and sweet smile have helped me through so many tough times. I will forever be grateful for you, love!

Elizabeth, you know I will always have your back, my sister. I have learned so much from you, and it has been a blessing having you in my life. I knew there was something special about you when we met at book club over a steaming hot pot of soup. I could have never guessed then that I had gained a true ride-or-die BFF that night. I cannot wait to hit up a spring training game with you again!

Boopie, hey there, babe! Thank you for being my fashion advisor and game time coach for my photoshoot. Thank you for your words of encouragement through this process. I love you, sister! Us California girls needs to stick together to keep it real! You truly are a fantastic and loyal friend. Thank you.

Emmy Beasties or Cabi Girls your love, acceptance, guidance, and support have been paramount for the years and years that we have been playing dress up and celebrating birthdays together. I love you each so dearly! We truly have the coolest girl gang!

My mentor, my friend, my older sister and former manager you know who you are. We didn't love one another right away. But once we put our differences aside and realized we are far more similar than we could have ever imagined, this beautiful friendship emerged. I love you! Thank you for your guidance and always serving as a reference for me.

My Nana, I love you. Thank you for using your direct line to God to send up so many prayers for me over the years. I am grateful for you, your humor, your artistic abilities, your cookies, and to be your Sunshine.

The amazing women who I have had the honor taking through the steps. Thank you for bringing me along on your beautiful journey. I love you!

Breakfast in the City ladies, thank you for your love and acceptance. I truly see God's love every time we get together to enjoy brunch and fellowship!

The OG's, The Originals, The Fun crowd. The amazing woman who showed me what acceptance and living without judgment looks like.

The insanely special women in my family, from all sides—my mothers', my fathers', and the family I married into-Thank You. I love you all. You have shown me what it looks like to be a strong woman, loving her family and living in faith. So much love to you especially, Auntie Em!

I love you with all of my heart, General Big Guy and Captain Underwear. You know who you are and I hope you know how grateful I am to call you mine. Thank you.

And to the alcoholics who I sit in meetings with, you have given me this life. You have taught me how to live with humility and show grace. I tried really hard to not be one of you. Now, I cannot imagine my life without you. You are my family. No matter where I go, there you are. I am eternally grateful for you.

AN OPEN LETTER

This is an open letter to the men who were such a large part of my life's transformation. I am including the boss I was working for during the darker days and Steve, my amazing attorney, and a very important figure you have already met in this homage.

I will start with Officer Young. Thank you. Thank you for treating me with respect and dignity both times we met. In 2014, when you took me from my home in pajamas, full of intense fear, you did the right thing. I know I justified it up and down for months after our meeting, but you were right. I was not sober when I drove home that night. Though you did not see me behind the wheel, and the gentleman who called you just wanted a payday, he too was right. I am sure you knew that this was not the first time I drove home after drinking. I also want to tell you that I honestly *was* blowing as hard as I could that night.

The breathalyzer machine we were using *was* broken. I promise, I was not conniving enough that night to only half-ass my blowing. I was scared. I arrived there with you in your police car. I didn't know where we were and what was going to happen. I know that the broken machine resulted in an automatic refusal, which resulted in a DUI charge for me, but I was insanely grateful that you brought me home that night.

To the true leader who gave me a safe place to be in recovery. Thank you for picking up the phone that night when I called. I was worried about making it to the meeting the next morning with an important client. Do you know how hard it was for me to tell you how stupid I had been? Do you know how embarrassing it was to have my car towed out of my driveway? Also, do you know the relief you gifted me when you told me not to worry, that you would take care of it. You always have "a guy." Thank you for introducing me to your guy and for helping me pay that guy to represent me. And for your support through that entire process. I know you said that was more than money well spent, but I have felt badly that nearly one year to the day I ended up in the same spot again. And you were there for me again. Thank you. You told me you hired me because you saw something in me that reminded you of yourself. That in and of itself is a huge compliment. I want you to know I will not ever forget your kindness and will for sure pay it forward.

And to Steve. You saw right through me, I think. After

years of working with people like me, of course you did! I wanted so badly for our working relationship to last only the amount of time it took for you to have my case pled down. I wanted so badly to do the right thing moving forward. In reality, I was always hungover when I met you monthly at the courthouse for those six months while we worked on my case. Thank you, nonetheless. You helped me move on, and it was my turn to take the reins and make a change. Your continued support, even to this day, sets you apart and for that you will always hold a special place in my heart.

Officer Young , we met again nearly one year later. If you knew, you never let on. This time, I thought I was so wise to refuse the breathalyzer. While I was held in the small downtown holding cell, sitting in a chair alone with my wrists handcuffed together, I thought about so much, including the fact that my injuries from the car accident really did hurt. I refused medical attention from the cuts and burns from the air bag in hopes that it would make it seem like I was fine—not too drunk, just a misguided driver. But a simple directional error does not land a local Seattleite in a situation where she's driving the wrong way down a one-way street into the side of another vehicle while "merging" into traffic. I am grateful for the quiet time we spent at the Harborview ER while we waited for my blood to be drawn. I heard things I had never witnessed in my life from the small space we shared while we waited for an RN to become available to draw my blood. Thank you for taking me home that night. You said it was due to the late hour and that there would probably be no room for me in the jail. Whether this was true or not, thank you! I will never forget the kind words you shared as you released me from your vehicle and I walked up to my front gate: "Make some changes. I would tell my own sister this. Get your life in order. I know it is something you can do." I know I only offered a simple thank you, but six years later I still remember it all. I have shared about your kindness many times. Thank you.

Finally, parole officer Pedro. You looked at me and my attorney and let us know that most people don't "make it" through the deferred prosecution process. You told me it was hard and that you had doubts about me. That's okay, you're allowed to have an opinion. I am sure that so many of your experiences leading up to that day brought you to that conclusion. I wish we'd had the opportunity to get to know one another, because I did make it through; it is possible. I know your job is hard, but please know that the system can work, and long-term recovery is possible. Thank you for all that you do. I will never forget you.

With gratitude and sincere thanks,
Sarah D. Cline-Alaimo

ABOUT THE AUTHOR

Sarah Alaimo is a Career Happiness Coach specializing in serving women in recovery. Sarah is also an Author, Healthcare Recruiter and Addiction Recovery Advocate.

A Southern California native massively deprived of sunshine while living in the Pacific Northwest, Alaimo loves her black Pomeranian, Baron, ice cream, the Los Angeles Angels of Anaheim baseball, travel adventures and her husband John.

Made in the USA
Columbia, SC
10 September 2023

22704587R00098